Renewing the Eucharist
Volume 2

Word

Renewing the Eucharist

Series editor: Stephen Burns

Volumes planned

1 *Journey*
GATHERING Richard Giles
WORD Nicola Slee
TABLE Ann Loades
SENDING Mark Ireland

2 *Word*
HEBREW SCRIPTURE Jo Bailey Wells
PSALMS Gordon Mursell
NEW TESTAMENT Joy Tetley
GOSPELS Andrew Gregory

3 *Table*
TAKING Lizette Larson-Miller
BLESSING David Stancliffe
BREAKING Alan Bartlett
GIVING John B. Thomson

4 *Prayer*
PRAISE Mark Earey
THANKSGIVING Stephen Platten
CONFESSION Harriet Harris
INTERCESSION John Pritchard

5 *Time*
CHRISTMAS CYCLE David Runcorn
EASTER CYCLE Ruth A. Meyers
ORDINARY TIME Ellen Clark-King
THE SAINTS Mark Pryce

for further information visit
www.canterburypress.co.uk

RENEWING THE EUCHARIST
Volume 2

Word

Jo Bailey Wells, Gordon Mursell,
Joy Tetley and Andrew Gregory

Series Editor:
Stephen Burns

© The Contributors 2009

First published in 2009 by the Canterbury Press Norwich
Editorial office
13–17 Long Lane, London EC1A 9PN

Canterbury Press is an imprint of Hymns Ancient and Modern Ltd
(a registered charity)
St Mary's Works, St Mary's Plain,
Norwich, NR3 3BH, UK

www.scm-canterburypress.co.uk

All rights reserved. No part of this publication may be reproduced,
stored in a retrieval system, or transmitted,
in any form or by any means, electronic, mechanical,
photocopying or otherwise, without the prior permission of
the publisher, Canterbury Press.

The Authors have asserted their right under the Copyright, Designs and
Patents Act, 1988, to be identified as the Authors of this Work

Scripture quotations are from the New Revised Standard Version of
the Bible, copyright © 1989 by the Division of Christian Education of
the National Council of the Churches of Christ in the USA, as found in
*Readings for the Assembly, Revised Common Lectionary Cycles A, B
and C*, edited by Gordon W. Lathrop and Gail Ramshaw, copyright ©
1995, 1996 and 1997 by Augsburg Fortress Press.

Extracts from *Common Worship: Services and Prayers for the Church
of England* are copyright © The Archbishops' Council 2000 and
reproduced by permission.

British Library Cataloguing in Publication data

A catalogue record for this book is available
from the British Library

ISBN 978-1-85311-888-3

Typeset by Regent Typesetting, London
Printed and bound by
CPI Bookmarque, Croydon, Surrey

Contents

Renewing the Eucharist: Orientation to the series   vii

The treasures of the Bible   1
Stephen Burns

Hebrew scripture   15
Jo Bailey Wells

Psalms   37
Gordon Mursell

New Testament   59
Joy Tetley

Gospels   82
Andrew Gregory

Appendix 1: A note on using this book to support preaching   105
Appendix 2: Sample questions for reflection and conversation   110

About the Contributors   114

Renewing the Eucharist
Orientation to the series

1 *Journey* 2 *Word* 3 *Table*
4 *Prayer* 5 *Time*

Renewing the Eucharist is a short series of small books on eucharistic spirituality. Each book offers concise, focused theological explorations of key liturgical themes intended to invite a readership across and beyond the Church of England. Now that the Church's *Common Worship* resources for the eucharist are authorized and employed in parishes, the *Renewing the Eucharist* series is a timely resource to help foster deepening liturgical formation of worshippers.

There are five volumes in the *Renewing the Eucharist* series. Each one consists of:

- an introductory essay by the editor,
- four thematic essays of 5,000 words each by leading thinkers on the key topic,
- a note on constructing lectionary sequences that will help to bring the themes of *Renewing the Eucharist* into preaching as part of eucharistic celebration, and

- some questions for thought for individual readers, or for conversation where the book is read in small groups.

Writers of the individual chapters present a core concern of theirs in a handful of pages, in accessible, non-technical language. 'What is the heart of this subject?' is the essential question they aim to address. Juxtaposed one to another, they aim to animate the connections between celebrating the eucharist and faithful Christian living, so that the spiritual practices of readers may be refreshed and emboldened.

The writers themselves come from a wide range of 'church styles' and theological traditions within the Church of England, with several writing from locations further afield. Each one writes from their own convictions; and the differences between them, as well as what they share, invite readers to refresh their own perspective on the journey through the liturgy, the central things of word and table, the modes and moods of prayer, and the unfolding of time – all gifts of grace.

The treasures of the Bible

STEPHEN BURNS

Scripture and liturgy closely bound

'Bible' is a plural word meaning 'books', though this point may not at first be obvious when picking up the books bound together in one collection. The origins of the collection, apart from each book that comprises it, are fascinating, and fragmentary. On the one hand, the beginnings of the Christian Bible relate to early Christian struggles to determine a relationship with the Jewish inheritance mediated by the Hebrew scriptures – texts that Jesus knew and prayed, preached and lived by. On the other hand, the origins of the Christian Bible relate to a complex and contested quest to determine a new collection of texts that would themselves give faithful witness to Jesus – drawing lines around what could and could not best be said about him.

Liturgy mediated both of these processes. Early Christian contexts of worship were the setting in which Christians carried over practices of attentiveness to Hebrew scriptures into freshly formed assemblies of their new group, 'church'. And over time, they withdrew from synagogue, shaped by the convictions of new texts that they regarded as complementing their inheritance in the Hebrew Bible, and they came to call that Hebrew Bible 'Old Testament'. At the same time, those texts that made their way into their 'New Testament' did so in large part because they came to find wide usage in assemblies of worship of the groups called church. Texts that could not command that wide liturgical use were not granted inclusion in the canon – the list of writings regarded as authoritative. At least some of the letters and texts that were in circulation, but which fell out of public use as the canon was defined, are available to us as the 'New Testament apocrypha', and contain among them strange and interesting things to set alongside the authorized documents that are familiar to Christian worshippers.[1] All of this is to say that the Bible was formed in the context of Christian worship.

Moreover, the Bible continues to be privileged as *the* key text in Christian worship: scripture and liturgy are closely bound together. There are indeed clues to this in scripture itself. Nehemiah's extraordinary account of reading to the people suggests at least one cluster of ways in which reading was experienced, and it has yielded its legacy to later Christian worship. In Nehemiah 8 we have a description of people gathering; of scrolls being read aloud by a person who was elevated on a platform; of prayer preceding reading; and of ritual gestures – the

---

[1] For a recent, attractive collection, see Marvin Meyer, 2005, *The Secret Gospels of Jesus: The Definitive Collection of Gnostic Gospels and Mystical Books about Jesus of Nazareth*, London: Darton, Longman and Todd.

lifting of hands, the bowing of heads – which surround the reading as reverence towards and response to what is heard. Perhaps most importantly, the text is interpreted: 'they gave the sense, so that the people understood the reading' (Nehemiah 8.8). Readers of *Word* will recognize the features of Nehemiah's account from their own and others' use of the Bible in Christian worship today: elevated reading to command attention, ritual gestures – perhaps kissing the gospel book[2] and crossing the forehead, lips and heart as an embodied prayer that the gospel reside within – and preaching.

'Modes' of 'word'

Within the New Testament itself, it is clear that Paul and other writers of letters expected that their words would be read in assemblies of the churches. And Jesus himself is remembered not only reading, preaching and interpreting the word (notably in Luke 4.16–20, when he announces with an emphatic 'today' that the meaning of the reading is fulfilled in his hearers' midst), but praying, perhaps singing, the word (some of his 'words from the cross' are themselves lines from the Psalms – his words at Mark 15.34 and Matthew 27.46 are from Psalm 22.1, and those at Luke 23.46 are from Psalm

---

[2] The Uniting Church in Australia, 2005, *Uniting in Worship 2*, Sydney: Uniting Church Press includes 'bluebrics' – margin notes of explanation that parallel red rubrics. One provocative bluebric notes for the former Methodists, Presbyterians and other heirs of the Reformation that Zwingli continued the practice of kissing the scriptures in his reformed liturgies!

31.5; see also Mark 14.26). Even more than that, Jesus is also remembered as enacting the word, one major part of which was in his table-companionship – which informs our eucharistic celebrations – which he saw as the outworking of ancient scriptural prophecy such as Isaiah 25:

> On this mountain the LORD of hosts will make for all peoples a feast of rich food, a feast of well-aged wines, of rich food filled with marrow, of well-aged wines strained clear. And the LORD will destroy on this mountain the shroud that is cast over all peoples, the sheet that is spread over all nations; the LORD will swallow up death for ever. Then the Lord GOD will wipe away the tears from all faces, and the disgrace of the chosen people God will take away . . . (Isaiah 25.6–8).[3]

So just as Jesus' preaching had an emphatic 'today' about it (Luke 4.20), so too his table practice was about beckoning divine presence in the here and now.

Perhaps for these as well as other reasons, Jesus himself came to be seen as 'word' of God, so that the luminous opening of John's gospel declares him 'word made flesh', 'who lived among us' (John 1.5, 14) while the First Letter of John evocatively speaks of a 'word' who has been seen and touched as well as heard, commanding all the senses (1 John 1.1–3). So Nicola Slee writes:

---

3 See Bruce Chilton, 1997, *Jesus' Prayer and Jesus' Eucharist: His Personal Practice of Spirituality*, Valley Forge, PA: Trinity Press International, for the significance of this text for Jesus.

Ultimately, the word for Christians is Jesus Christ, the beloved, who comes to us in flesh and blood as the manifestation of God's truth: a human being who shows us what it means to live God's truth and seek God's way; a word-in-action, a word translated into terms we can handle, touch, hear and see (1 John 1.1–3) – not, in the first place, therefore, a text, a doctrine or a concept, but a life, a life that engaged all the realities of our human lives (pain, desire, hunger, thirst, glory, suffering) and revealed God in the midst of them . . .[4]

Yet scripture itself came to be regarded as 'word of God' in a derivative sense, as indicated by the kind of statement made at the end of scripture readings in the liturgy:

The Word of the Lord.
Thanks be to God.

Comparison may be made with Jeremiah 2.4, or variants such as 'The word of life' or 'Holy wisdom, holy word'.[5] The mechanics or dynamics of 'inspiration' – the

---

4 Nicola Slee, 2008, 'Word', Stephen Burns, ed., *Renewing the Eucharist, Volume 1, Journey*, Norwich: Canterbury Press, pp. 36–61, 37.

5 These particular variants are drawn from the lectionary resources used for Bible quotations in this series, Gordon W. Lathrop and Gail Ramshaw, eds, 1995–7, *Readings for the Assembly*, Minneapolis, MN: Fortress Press, three volumes; see p. viii in the introduction to each volume. The Church of England, 2002, *New Patterns for Worship*, London: Church House Publishing, pp. 107–23, suggests a range of such responses and models means of varying such affirmations of the words of scripture. See note 5 on p. 105.

doctrinal notion which affirms that scripture is in some sense, in some way 'God breathed', given – are wisely undefined by most Christians, however. We affirm the mysterious sense that the word does indeed 'touch' persons, while we are also open to the very real experience of struggle with at least some of the texts at least some of the time. Hence, how God speaks through the Bible is perhaps best imagined in analogy to a conversation, as opposed to monologue, where tradition, diverse interpreters and, in one way or another, others as well as ourselves are honoured with space to help determine meanings for us.[6] And it needs to be remembered that the scripture is in any case richly comprised of different media as multivalent as spoken and written words: images, symbols, and songs, each of which funds the wider environment in which worship happens and scripture is read, inspiring art – visual, musical, architectural, and in various modes – in many church buildings, and which may in their own turn help persons to read the Bible, opening up the text in pictures, space and sound. So directly and more indirectly the Bible provides a wealth of resources upon which liturgy draws. Turning to the 'index of biblical references' in any volume of *Common Worship* to see something of the ways in which scripture provides and shapes texts for prayer is itself instructive.[7]

---

6 Arnold Browne helpfully speaks about the Bible itself as a 'conversation of voices', Arnold Browne, 1997, 'Yesterday, Today and Forever', Stephen Platten, Graham James and Andrew Chandler, eds, *New Soundings: Essays on Developing Tradition*, London: Darton, Longman & Todd, pp. 13–35, 35.

7 Note the helpful collation of texts under the heading 'scrip-

Lectionary patterns

Among early accounts of worship outside the Bible itself, perhaps the most significant is that of Justin Martyr in mid-second-century Rome describing reading from 'records of the apostles or the writings of the prophets' before a preacher's invitation 'into the pattern of these beautiful things'.[8] These readings may well have corresponded to what we know today as New Testament and Old Testament.

In Anglican worship today, as with many other traditions, the reading of the Bible is patterned by use of a lectionary, that is, an agreed series of readings, throughout the year. The second appendix of this volume introduces some of the patterns, freedoms and constraints that are part of the *Common Worship* lectionary, which is itself a close amendment of a lectionary shared by a widening number of Protestant Churches – the Revised Common Lectionary (RCL) – which in turn developed out of ecumenical reflection on Roman Catholic use of their Lectionary for Mass. The Lectionary for Mass itself developed from the luminous conviction of Roman Catholic bishops at the Second Vatican Council who wished 'the treasures of the Bible . . . to be opened up more lavishly so that a richer fare may be provided for the faithful at the table of God's word'.[9]

---

ture and worship' in 2006, *Evangelical Lutheran Worship*, Minneapolis, MN: Augsburg Fortress Press, pp. 1154–1159.

8 Cited in Stephen Burns, 2006, *SCM Studyguide to Liturgy*, London: SCM Press, p. 18. See discussion of Justin in Stephen Burns, 2008, 'The Journey through the Liturgy', Stephen Burns, ed., *Renewing the Eucharist, Volume 1, Journey*, pp. 1–13, 8.

9 *Sacrosanctum concilium*, 53.

The RCL is a three-yearly cycle, the gospel readings across each year focusing in turn on the gospels of Matthew, Mark and Luke. The gospel of John is used across the three years, interspersed with readings from the gospel that is the focus of the year, although John is especially likely to appear at Easter, Christmas or other 'golden times' of the calendar.

This means that on any given Sunday, across any number of Christian traditions, in many parts of the world, Christians are often to be found opening the same scripture passages in their assemblies. So Roman Catholics in Chile, Lutherans in Sweden and Anglicans in Australia might all be reading the same texts.

The appeal of a lectionary seems to be broadening, given that traditions that previously had not adopted set patterns of readings, Methodists or Baptists, for example, now find the RCL either available or commended in the liturgical provisions of their tradition.[10] This turn to the lectionary means that it is a quite remarkable feature – and expression – of ecumenism.

Not all traditions use the lectionary in exactly the same way,[11] although the RCL provides for an Old Testament reading, a psalm, a New Testament reading and a gospel

---

10 See, for example, 1999, *Methodist Worship Book*, Peterborough: Methodist Publishing House, pp. 521, 565–600 and 2005, *Gathering for Worship: Patterns and Prayers for the Community of Disciples*, Norwich: Canterbury Press, p. 350.

11 An example is the way that 2003, *Worship from the United Reformed Church*, does not always specify use of a gospel reading other than as an option among 'New Testament Reading(s)'. See pp. 6, 21 ('A reading from a Gospel (and/or other New Testament book)'), p. 43, etc.

reading at celebrations of the eucharist. In the *Common Worship* lectionary, as in many other traditions, they are read in that order, so that the effect is as it were to 'give Jesus the last word' by using the gospel as a focusing lens on the rest of the readings. It should also be noted that the sermon need not necessarily follow the gospel reading (though this is the default position), but may in fact fall before or after any of the readings.[12]

The pattern of readings: Old Testament, psalm, New Testament, gospel

In this volume of *Renewing the Eucharist*, the four writers following this introductory essay take in turn the streams from which the four lectionary readings at the eucharist are drawn: Old Testament, psalms, New Testament, gospels. The ways in which they choose to approach their particular topic are related, but not the same – which is itself one signal of the wealth of the subject matter that makes the Bible bear repeated attention Sunday after Sunday.

In 'Hebrew scripture', Jo Bailey Wells begins by emphasizing connections between scripture and liturgy – an emphasis found in the writings of the other writers, notably in Joy Tetley's chapter. Jo is an Old Testament scholar, having been both chaplain and dean of Clare College and then tutor in Old Testament at Ridley Hall, Cambridge, before moving to Duke University, North Carolina, where she now teaches Bible and ministry and

---

12 See note 4, *New Patterns for Worship*, p. 14.

directs the Anglican studies programme. She is, then, one acquainted with ways in which scriptures are engaged in the practices of worship across different kinds of setting, and not least among persons in formation for ministry. In her essay here, Jo shows how eucharistic practices grew out of Jewish liturgical practices, which were themselves ways of participating in Hebrew scripture. Passover is central to her explorations, and, she suggests, can model a way for Christians at the eucharist to 'glimpse God's story from the inside'. She explores different genres of literature within the Old Testament, is sensitive to the question of how the relationship between the New Testament and Hebrew scripture might be conceived – suggesting a cautious 'supersession' with important caveats and subtleties – and proposes a way of framing the diversity of material to be found in the Hebrew scriptures within a broad framework. Notably, Jo's essay commends some reading practices – with the heart, in communion – and with reference to the latter she touches on some contemporary controversies in global Anglicanism. In the face of such controversies, she regards the diversity of the Old Testament as a resource for rising to 'the challenge . . . to treasure every priceless voice'.

Gordon Mursell, the Bishop of Stafford, follows Jo's essay with his own on one Old Testament book especially privileged in Christian worship – the Psalms. He provides a spacious framework for approaching the collection of 150 Hebrew songs, the words of which Jo Bailey Wells had earlier described as 'passionate, confident, mystified, wondrous, brutal, proud, grieved, desperate'. Gordon chooses to focus in on one psalm in particular: Psalm 73 – interestingly a psalm that does not feature in the three-year *Common Worship* lectionary for the eucharist (it appears in Proper 11, year B, for the second service, where it may be shortened to just verses 21–28).[13] Gordon draws attention to the context from which the psalms come to us – the worship of the Jewish people – as well as the contexts in which Christian people might lean into the Psalms today, and not least in demanding circumstances – perhaps as Jesus was remembered remembering psalms in his bleakest experiences. Throughout, Gordon holds in creative tension ways in which the psalter might relate to corporate and individual experience, public and personal happenings. So his essay makes mention of AIDS, eco-spirituality, persons and creation in travail, widely shared issues and concerns as well as intimate encounter with divine presence. As readers familiar with Gordon's many studies in spiritual practices might well expect, he offers a reading of the psalms that is fully engaged with contemporary life.[14] In his essay here, as elsewhere, he manifests a deep and broad love of spirituality, which so many of his other writings have done so much to help foster in others.[15] His essay also anticipates a forthcoming

---

13 See 2000, *Common Worship: Services and Prayers for the Church of England*, London: Church House Publishing, pp. 567, 590.

14 Note Gordon Mursell, 2006, 'Praying the Gospels: Spirituality and Worship', Stephen C. Barton, ed., *The Cambridge Companion to the Gospels*, Cambridge: Cambridge University Press, pp. 245–63.

15 See, for example, Gordon Mursell, ed., 2001, *The Story of*

volume of *Renewing the Eucharist* on prayer, in that he discusses different ways of praying. To the 'modes and moods' discussed in that later volume – praise, thanks, confession and intercession – Gordon introduces the genre of lament, which is not well represented in eucharistic liturgies.[16] As such, he offers a welcome corrective to weightings in this series over all.

Especially complementing Jo Bailey Wells's concern to make links between scripture and liturgy, Joy Tetley, in the third essay following, draws attention to ways in which eucharistic liturgy is permeated by New Testament phraseology and allusion. And just as Gordon Mursell focused in on one psalm, Joy focuses in on one book, the 'comparatively neglected' letter to the Hebrews, an 'intriguing, adventurous and powerful work'. Joy explores ideas of Jesus as high priest and of the new covenant, in which 'pain and joy are inseparably linked' in 'God's passion for the world'. She places special stress on the kinds of education that might enable persons to be excited, rather than baffled or bored, by the scripture readings in Church of England worship.

Christian Spirituality: Two Thousand Years, from East to West, Oxford: Lion.

16 See also Gordon Mursell, 2005, *Praying in Exile*, London: Darton, Longman & Todd, pp. 39–61. *Uniting in Worship 2* includes lament as the main feature of the gathering rite in its Second Service of the Lord's Day, pp. 200–202. *New Patterns for Worship* provides a discrete service, 'Facing Pain', pp. 443–48, and *Gathering for Worship* includes some resources, pp. 318–22. On liturgical lament, see also Anita Monro and Stephen Burns, 2008, 'Faithful Prayer on Parched Land: On Being Asked to Provide Liturgies for a Time of Drought', *Uniting Church Studies* 14, pp. 51–64.

Andrew Gregory, Chaplain and Fellow of University College, Oxford, follows with an essay on the gospels, making the most explicit connections of any of the authors in this volume with material covered by essays in the earlier volume of *Renewing the Eucharist – Journey*. He does so in that he begins and ends his chapter with reflections on the Lucan memory of the risen Jesus' encounter with two disciples on the road to Emmaus (Luke 24.11–35) – an encounter in which the risen one is known as the scriptures are opened and bread is broken. In Volume 1, this Lucan story was identified as the key piece of biblical material shaping durable patterns of eucharistic celebration, strongly affirmed in contemporary ecumenical consensus. Andrew also draws on his own extensive work on 'the fourfold gospel'[17] to consider that we inherit from the Christian tradition four gospels, rather than either one or many more, as well as how these four are used in contemporary lectionary patterns and how these gospel readings relate to other readings in lectionary sequences used at the eucharist. In doing so, he raises critical questions about the lectionary more than other writers in this present volume, and lifts up some Reformed reserve about some lectionary dynamics.[18] While affirming the 'gospel-based Christological focus' of lectionary patterns of readings, he

---

17 See Andrew Gregory, 2005, *Four Witnesses, One Gospel?*, Cambridge: Grove and Andrew Gregory, ed., 2006, *The Fourfold Gospel Commentary*, London: SPCK.

18 See John Goldingay, 1999, 'Canon and Lection', Bryan D. Spinks and Iain R. Torrance, eds, *To Glorify God: Essays on Modern Reformed Liturgy*, Edinburgh: T&T Clark, pp. 85–97, to which Andrew refers in his essay.

commends other ways of reading the scriptures alongside the way that they are opened in Christian assembly: 'we need to read the whole Bible . . . for ourselves' – a point that can be allied to Joy Tetley's call for the church to take seriously its task of education.

In their pieces for this collection, each author draws on their own particular expertise to open out their topic. There are shifting levels of focus between overview and particular foci, from attention to a kind of 'five-act play' being imagined to do at least some justice to the trajectory of scripture, to zooming in on a single chapter for constant re-orientation. There are different complementary emphases: for example, Jo Bailey Wells on 'absorbing the story . . . "playing" oneself into its outworking', Joy Tetley on 'performance' of scripture[19] by preachers and others in their turn. Each in their own way asserts the importance of looking at the Bible as some sort of whole, as this volume itself attempts to do, in however cursory a fashion. And each in their own way celebrates the Bible's capacity to fuel a living spirituality centred on encounter with divine presence, known not least in renewal at the eucharist.

---

19 See Stephen C. Barton, 2001, 'New Testament Interpretation as Performance', *Life Together: Family, Sexuality and Community in the New Testament and Today*, Edinburgh: T&T Clark, pp. 223–50.

Hebrew scripture

JO BAILEY WELLS

Participation in the scriptures

The eucharist makes no sense without the Old Testament, liturgically or theologically. Liturgically: because the Christian habits of worship have developed from Jewish practices of prayer and praise. Theologically: because the first eucharist, 'the last supper', was a celebration of the Passover, the annual festival at which the Jews recall the defining events of their salvation. Although the church is constituted by a 'resurrection people', a 'Pentecost people', the events of Christ's passion and resurrection and the outpouring of the Spirit at Pentecost make little sense without the background into which they belong and to which they respond. Indeed, vast stretches of the New Testament may be understood only through the metaphors and themes that framed the imagination of early Christians immersed in Hebrew scripture. If contemporary Christians are tempted to skip the Hebrew scriptures, their Old Testament – as commonly as the Old Testament reading is cut from a Sunday service – they are liable to cut off the branch on which they sit.

This chapter is not simply about engaging scripture, and the Old Testament in particular, within the liturgy: it begins with an explanation of the way in which liturgy *is* a participation in the scriptures.

Re-living the past

The Israelites took very seriously the need to cultivate the skills of remembering. They are commanded to 'remember you were slaves in Egypt' so that they never fail to appreciate the gift of their freedom. They are encouraged to remember 'your father was a wandering Aramean' in order to find compassion for the needy. And, during periods of disaster or discouragement – most notably in the exile – the act of remembering becomes a radical act of defiance, a means of rekindling a reality that was otherwise denied, vital to their very survival as the people of God.

It was during the exile that the Jewish people organized the writings relating to the foundation of Israel. They also recorded many of the psalms. They developed habits of telling and re-telling these writings – the use of mnemonics and acrostics for memorizing psalms, the organized regular reading of scripture at Sabbath gatherings – in order to initiate each new generation into the identity and calling of the people of God. These might correspond to contemporary habits of learning Bible verses and using a lectionary in church today.

The annual enactment of the Passover is the most vivid and most important habit of all: a habit that we follow, in fact, whenever we celebrate the eucharist. But the problem with habit – when it becomes routine – is that we are prone to miss its significance. The recitation of the eucharistic prayer represents the corporate recollection of the defining events of our salvation. By recalling these events, Sunday by Sunday, we are rehearsing the story within which we sit – ideally to the point where we wholly inhabit it.

Until I visited India over Christmas a few years ago, I used to think that nativity plays were a quaint habit for the sake of amusing the parents and grandparents of small children, or at least for the kindling of sentimental spirit at Christmas. But around a variety of workplaces and college environments in Delhi my eyes were opened to the opportunity of this genre for enabling participants – all adults, of varying faiths and backgrounds – to re-enact the story and enter into its significance for themselves. Friends, colleagues and family were eager to have a role, to participate in the Christian festival of Christmas and re-create the drama for the community – whether (individually) they called themselves Christians and claimed this story personally or not. In so doing they were entering into it whether or not they realized it – exploring what sort of person Mary was, what sort of circumstances God chose, offering imaginative cultural interpretations and hilarious renditions. Nativity plays offered a way of absorbing the story of Jesus' birth by 'playing' oneself into its outworking – and thus (sometimes unintentionally) finding oneself a part.

The Christian practice of eucharist – as with the Jewish habit of Passover – offers the same kind of opportunity: 'Do this in remembrance of me', Jesus said. We remember by doing, by re-living and continually repeating the events surrounding the Last Supper. Such habits of remembering are borrowed from the Jews, who rehearsed the events of the Passover each year in order to teach the children and their children's children, that 'it was not to your fathers and forefathers that . . . but to you . . .'.

The Passover Seder follows a set pattern, which takes place at the family dinner table. There are readings and prayers, and there is symbolic action – with bread and wine, with bitter herbs and salt water, and finally with a feast of roast lamb. Over the generations, a liturgy is established and rehearsed time after time, where all the family participates, with roles assigned from the youngest child to the oldest adults. The re-enactment invites the involvement of the people of God at every stage of life and with a range of sensory engagement – listening, voicing, watching, tasting, smelling – so that all the participants become aligned with the story of God's salvation – its history beginning in Egypt and its promises ending in the new Jerusalem. Thus, the enactment, though rooted in past events, encompasses present reality and directs the gaze to yet greater things to come. In the process, a community is, literally, 're-membered' (that is, the members are newly joined in common cause). In recalling the past, the community's imagination for God is re-kindled.

The Old Testament offers Christians a model for remembering – for re-telling and re-living past events in order that they become present to a generation far removed, in order that they become real for a people who are exiled, in order that they re-member a people who have been knit together through the stories they share. That system of remembering demands full, flexible, faithful participation – it requires of us that we take our part in the 'play' – so that we may begin to glimpse God's story from the inside.

Language for God's praise

It is the Old Testament that also supplies so much of the vocabulary with which we praise God. The chief end of all human beings, indeed all creation, is to glorify God and enjoy God forever. The book of Psalms, in particular, offers the language with which to begin: a set of hymns that have functioned in Hebrew worship and form the most foundational 'hymnbook' of the church. In the psalms, words that were originally directed *to* God in the form of prayers of praise or lament – passionate, confident, mystified, wondrous, brutal, proud, grieved, desperate – have, through their incorporation into the biblical canon, become words *from* God that legitimately and authoritatively shape our habits of petition and complaint. Here, then, are suitable models for confessing sin, for voicing grief, for acknowledging a new leader, for leading intercessions – as well as for finding words with which to begin to express God's glory.

The most elemental is, surely, 'hallelujah'. This Hebrew word has become a virtually universal expression of praise to God – both in written liturgy as well as through spontaneous habit across countless languages. Actually, it is originally an imperative statement, an injunction that urges a gathering of people to praise God – literally, 'All of you, praise God!'[20] There are other lines stemming from the Old Testament that form an integral part of our eucharistic liturgy, most prominently the *sanctus*: 'Holy, holy, holy is the LORD of hosts; the whole earth is full of the glory of the LORD' (Isaiah 6.3). This is the song of the angels around God's throne with which worshippers are invited to join, a song first heard – or glimpsed – by Isaiah during the vision in which he understood God's glory, recoiled at his own unworthiness yet heard God calling him to service.

The church's practice of borrowing lines from the Old Testament to praise God begins in the New Testament. Both 'hallelujah' and 'holy, holy, holy' are themselves found quoted in the book of Revelation.[21] This underlines the way in which Christians receive and appropriate the Hebrew scriptures. The place where the psalm traditionally belongs in the eucharistic liturgy – after the Old Testament reading and before the Epistle, often sung as a 'gradual' – underlines the role of this timeless language of praise, expressing the unchangeability of God while at the same time transitioning us from the horizon of a former era to the New Testament world within which the church belongs.

---

20 Literally, *hallelu-* is the second person masculine plural imperative of the Hebrew verb *hallel*, which means to praise joyfully or to boast. The second part, *-jah*, is a shortened form of the name for God, YHWH, often translated as 'the LORD'.

21 The Hebrew 'hallelujah' is transliterated (rather than translated) into the Greek text as 'allelouia', which explains the alternative forms that the church has received, hallelujah and alleluia.

Has the Old Testament been superseded?

It is clear from the very name Christians commonly use for the Hebrew scriptures, 'the Old Testament', that we read them in the light of a sequel. It is vital, though not inevitable, that we seek to understand all that came before Christ in the light of Christ, and leading to Christ. This is the sense in which the first testament is 'Old' – not outdated in the sense of being inferior, not unnecessary in the sense of being replaced, but earlier and pre-dating an event through which it is now re-read with new perspective.

This is the sense – a limited sense – in which we may say the Old Testament has been superseded. We do not set it aside – as with an old model of computer once we have a newer one; rather its canonical status continues (as 2 Timothy 3.16 has it, 'all scripture is inspired by God and is useful for' a number of things) and we continue to find in this earlier testament, testimony to the life of faith. The sixth article of faith set forth in the Thirty-nine Articles of Anglican tradition affirms that 'Scripture containeth all things necessary to salvation' and lists 66 books of the Bible – both Old and New Testaments – to underline the significance of them all for salvation. Article Seven continues: 'The Old Testament is not contrary to the New: for both in the Old and New Testament everlasting life is offered to Mankind by Christ, who is the only Mediator between God and Man, being both God and Man.'

Thus, we continue to read the Old Testament as the church, perhaps most definitively when we gather for eucharist: and yet we do not read the Old Testament alone but in sequence with New Testament readings. Oftentimes there are four scripture readings in the Liturgy of the Word, the second part of the journey through the liturgy.[22] Two readings are taken from the Old Testament and two from the New: first 'the Old Testament reading', then an appointed Psalm (which is sometimes sung), then 'the New Testament reading' and then 'the Gospel'. Just as the Liturgy of the Word gives pre-eminence to the gospels within the New Testament, so it gives particular prominence to the Psalter within the Old Testament. And although a preacher may choose to focus on any one of the readings, in the public reading of scripture each is heard in the light of other parts of scripture. That is to say, we seek to interpret scripture 'inter-textually' – where each text contributes to the understanding of the rest.

A book of prophecy and promise?

The Thirty-nine Articles beg the question of how salvation is offered through the Old Testament as well as through the New Testament. Richard Hooker spoke of the way in which the Old Testament reveals Christ by pointing the way to him as the one who fulfils what is promised. Certainly, when we read from luminous pas-

---

22 See 2000, *Common Worship: Services and Prayers for the Church of England*, London: Church House Publishing, p. x and Stephen Burns, 'The Journey Through the Liturgy', Stephen Burns, ed., *Renewing the Eucharist, Volume 1, Journey* Norwich: Canterbury Press, pp. 1–13.

sages of the prophets – most notably Isaiah – during Advent and Holy Week, we may recognize passages that point to Christ and which are only fully and finally fulfilled in Christ. But it is harder to recognize the same level of anticipation and promise in stories from Genesis, or legal codes in Leviticus, or wisdom in Proverbs.

We are prone to be frustrated by the seeming irrelevance of much of the Old Testament if we read it only with an eye to it pointing to Christ. Indeed, even with books like Isaiah I suggest we miss a lot of the depth within the text if we do not allow the text to speak first and foremost to its own context, whether that is its historical context in Israel or its literary context within the Old Testament. What is more, only one stretch of the Old Testament presents itself as prophecy (from Isaiah to Malachi): the other sections are traditionally termed the Law (Genesis through to Deuteronomy) and the Writings (a more miscellaneous collection including the historical books and the wisdom literature). These collections themselves encompass a wide variety of genres: the 'Law', for example, consists mainly of narrative, and even the legal codes are set within a narrative frame. The Writings contain narrative, and poetry, proverbs and history: but even the history is narrated like a story – it is a recounting of events rather than a presentation of 'facts'. Within the books of the Prophets, there is both poetry and prose. Some of this is exhortatory, some is condemnatory and some is apocalyptic. How we read this material must depend on the nature of the material.

And, just as with any book, *how* we read it is determined by *why* we read it. We scan a telephone directory in search of a very particular piece of information; we enjoy poetry for its imaginative expression; we are held by a mystery novel to find out what happens; we study a textbook to understand the principles of a subject; we read history to learn about a previous era. We might legitimately read the Old Testament for any and all of these purposes. Yet, within the context of a confessional community of believers, and focused in the corporate act of worship, we share a wider, bigger purpose: to learn about God, and the life of faith under God. As the 'Collect for Purity', used in the gathering rite of the *Common Worship* eucharist, puts it, 'that we may perfectly love you and worthily magnify your holy name'.[23]

This is why we read the New Testament also. Through the combined testimonies of God's ways in the past, we understand the God we worship and serve in the present. We learn that God – as with Jesus Christ – 'is the same yesterday, today and forever'. It is *not* the case, as is popularly supposed, that the God of the Old Testament is a God of judgement, whereas the God of the New Testament is a God of love. The God revealed as YHWH to Israel and the God revealed through Jesus Christ are one and the same: the God of love *and* justice, judgement *and* grace. The 'gospel' of the Old Testament may be less evident to the casual eye – and the texts of judgement more extensive – yet there is good news in both testaments. God's prerogative in both testaments is to bless, to save and to call. Each testament hinges on the redemption of God's people. Just as the New Testa-

---

23 *Common Worship*, p. 168.

ment hinges on the events of Christ's life, death and resurrection through which God's people receive full and final forgiveness and the gift of the Holy Spirit at Pentecost, so the Old Testament hinges on the events of the exodus by which God's people are rescued from slavery in Egypt and brought to a relationship of covenant and freedom in the promised land.

Thus, we find in the Old Testament far more than a set of promises awaiting fulfilment. We find out about the God who calls and re-calls people to follow, the God who goes to great lengths to rescue a suffering people, the God who patiently challenges and renews God's wayward, forgetful people. And we find out about people who have ventured out in faith; people who have re-ordered their priorities according to God's call, and those who have tried to follow God but failed. In the Old Testament we find paradigms of faith and faithfulness – as well as faithlessness and foolishness – to guide and inform our own journeys. Perhaps some of them also function to horrify or amuse – such that when read in a service, we might most aptly follow them with the response re-phrased into a taunting tease, '*This* is the Word of the Lord!' or the ironic question, 'This is the Word of the *Lord*?' Certainly, the Old Testament demands a sense of humour and adventure!

The story of the Old Testament

It is helpful – particularly when it comes to some of the more unusual or complicated texts – to know where a particular passage fits in to the whole. Hence, a well-thought-out sentence of explanation and introduction before a reading during a service of worship can help to situate a congregation within the wider story.[24]

Much of the Old Testament may be recounted as a single story of Israel's dealings with God,[25] even though the books of the Old Testament do not follow a neat narrative or chronological sequence.[26] In a nutshell, the story would begin with Abraham in Genesis 12, God's call to Abraham to leave home and family to 'go . . . to the land that I will show you . . . I will bless you . . . so that you will be a blessing . . . and in you all the families of the earth shall be blessed' (Genesis 12.3). Genesis follows the thread of this promise of blessing, through Abraham's children and grandchildren, through the ups and downs of marital complexity, sibling rivalry and political strife. Abraham's descendants land up in Egypt, in slavery, where God's promises would appear to have been thwarted by the abuses of the Pharaoh: the bearers enslaved, prevented from nurturing descendants and from experiencing blessing.

So Exodus begins with the problem and the challenge

---

24 Note further ideas in *New Patterns for Worship*, p. 100.

25 For an example of the Old Testament recast as a continuous story, see Walter Wangerin, 1998, *The Book of God*, London: Lion Hudson.

26 Equally, some books function to counter the dominant narrative. Walter Brueggemann has helpfully cast the Old Testament literature into the three categories of testimony, dispute and advocacy, showing how they each relate to the narrative of God with Israel. See Walter Brueggemann, 2005, *Theology of the Old Testament: Testimony, Dispute, Advocacy*, Minneapolis, MN: Fortress Press.

HEBREW SCRIPTURE

– and God's call to Moses to lead the people out of Egypt. The great escape is traumatic, not least because the journey through the desert to the land God promised is tough. The journey is spiritual as well as physical, a place where God calls the people to be a nation and prepares them for life in the promised land. In particular, God makes a covenant with them at Sinai: 'if you obey my voice and keep my covenant, you shall be my treasured possession . . . a realm of priests and a holy nation' (Exodus 19.5–6). They readily agree, and receive the laws and stipulations that go along with the covenant commitment, described in the remainder of Exodus and Leviticus, so that 'you shall be holy, for I the LORD your God am holy' (Leviticus 19.2). The book of Deuteronomy provides a second account of this vital stage of Israel's formation – as if to underline the importance of getting it right – as the prelude to further historical narratives in which Israel claims the promised land and settles it.[27] Chronicles competes with Samuel–Kings to interpret the triumphs and defeats of the monarchic period of Israel's history in which there is a division of Israel into two kingdoms and – inexorably it seems – further downfall, leading to exile.

Other Old Testament books are less narrative in approach. Yet both major and minor prophets – some pre-exile, some during exile, and some post-exile – relate to this narrative by their function to remind the people of Israel of their core commitments – of the covenant and its consequences, as laid down in the Pentateuch[28]

---

27 Joshua, Judges, Samuel, Kings.
28 'The Pentateuch' describes the first five books of the Old

– in order to urge them to renew their lives in repentance and faithfulness. Although prophecy contains an element of prediction – fore-telling the future – this usually comes in the wider context of forth-telling, that is, naming present circumstances, in the manner of a preacher who has a word to deliver to the people and expects a real-time response.

One other major category of Old Testament literature is that of wisdom. Some psalms, and the books of Proverbs, Job, Ecclesiastes and the Song of Songs, operate very differently from the narrative strands of Genesis–Chronicles or the prophecies of Isaiah–Malachi. Rather than tell a story, the approach of wisdom is to observe in creation the ways of the creator. As well as this very wide purview, wisdom also values insight gleaned from intricate and intimate human experience of family life and domestic circumstance, as if to suggest in very practical and sometimes playful terms (for example, in Proverbs): 'This is the way to live. Try it and see.'[29] And the more sceptical texts (for example, Ecclesiastes) answer back in sobering tone, 'We did. And it didn't.' Wisdom represents a mode of literature to be read slowly and pondered, like poetry – to be enjoyed for its language and observation rather than its didactic substance. It also gives us permission to be confused, to raise awk-

---

Testament, from Genesis to Deuteronomy. Like the gospels in the New Testament, these books function as the foundational narratives, which are assumed by the rest of the testament that follows after.

29 See Proverbs 8.5: 'Come, eat of my bread and drink of the wine I have mixed. Lay aside immaturity and live, and walk in the way of insight.'

ward questions, to admit when life's pieces do not add up. At the same time, the wisdom literature draws us back to the overarching frame within which the story of Israel sits (Genesis 1—11): that of a creator-God who delights in creating and who is responsible for the whole of creation – not just a single people. In fact, as the promises to Abraham make clear (Genesis 12.3), God called a particular people not for their own sake – as if marking a change of policy – but for the sake of the whole world.

Reading with the heart

At the outset of every eucharist, the Collect for Purity beckons participants to open their hearts to God.[30] And at the outset of the eucharistic prayer, the dialogue known as the *sursum corda* summons the body of believers to 'Lift up your hearts'. How do we use our hearts in the reading of scripture?

Both in the Old and New Testaments, in Hebrew and Greek, the biblical term 'heart' refers to what we would more commonly call the imagination.[31] Both in the Liturgy of the Word and in the Liturgy of the Sacrament the imagination is called upon in worship: and perhaps

---

30 'Almighty God, to whom all hearts are open, all desires known . . .'

31 Garrett Green, 1989, *Imagining God: Theology and the Religious Imagination*, San Francisco: Harper & Row, pp.109–10. Quoted by Ellen F. Davis, 2003, 'Teaching the Bible Confessionally in the Church', Ellen F. Davis and Richard B. Hays, eds, *The Art of Reading Scripture*, Grand Rapids: Eerdmans, pp. 9–26, see p. 11.

the need is never as great as when it comes to hearing God's word from the Old Testament.

To most of us, especially in the West, the Old Testament feels 'foreign'.[32] It requires an exercise of the imagination – which includes a willingness to read slowly – to cross the 'culture gap' and engage the world of sacrifice and symbolism, patriarchs and prophets, manna and mystery. It also requires an exercise of faith to live with uncertain impressions and resist glib interpretation. I can think of no other answer to the question, 'Why is the Old Testament so hard to understand?' than to presume that it is in the act of living with a passage – even of wrestling with it – that we learn to engage more deeply with the God who stands behind it. In the very act of engaging the literary complexity of the material we are carried more deeply into the theological realm, and into the heart of God.

Yet exactly where the Old Testament seems least attractive, harsh to the taste, or indigestible, the perceived need of many Christian preachers (if indeed such passages are read at all in worship) is to *explain* them. The danger is that to explain may be to reduce – whereas the aim of worship (including the sermon) is to train the eyes of the heart to see what is not ordinarily visible, and thus to see our own circumstances and the possibilities for our lives differently in the light of that seeing. If the Old Testament addresses itself to our imagination, then preachers serve it best when they do not try to explain

---

32 I have, incidentally, taught in Sudan, where it seemed to me that students loved the Old Testament precisely because Leviticus, for example, related so *closely* to their world.

and define so much as open up and let loose – to allow the text to do the work of deepening theological insight and renewing moral vision in the church.[33]

Reading with the heart, then, is likely a demanding exercise, and one that is incumbent on us all, not just on the preacher. As we allow the demands of the text to work on us, so it is – in my experience – that we start to dwell within the text, to relate to its characters, to inhabit its world, to be held by its tensions and even to be content *not* to understand it. In such circumstances, the text is not resolved – it continues to work within us – so long as we can resist the temptation of premature explanation and application. As with the actors in a nativity play, so we find ourselves more fully inside God's unfolding plan of salvation – even (perhaps especially) if we are tantalized by it. And God's plan, outlined and substantiated by both testaments, may be characterized as a five-act play, each act describing a decisive act of God for the sake of the world, as follows: (I) Creation, (II) Israel, (III) Jesus, (IV) Church and (V) End.[34] This five-act play helpfully brings us to realize that we are indeed actors within it: and that, though the pages of scripture are closed, the play has not ended

---

33 I am indebted here to Ellen F. Davis, 2008, 'No Explanations in the Church', Carol M. Bechtel, ed., *Touching the Altar: The Old Testament for Christian Worship*, Grand Rapids: Eerdmans, pp. 95–122. The title of Davis's chapter is borrowed from a sign to tour guides as one enters the site of Gethsemane, p. 96.

34 I am indebted to N. T. Wright for this idea, which has subsequently found development in Samuel Wells, 2004, *Improvisation: The Drama of Christian Ethics*, London: SPCK.

– even though Christians are those privileged to know how it will end.

Reading in communion

If we are to listen with the heart and take our place in the unfolding drama of God's action, then we need one another. We need one another not least to help fire our imagination – so that many sets of eyes and ears may spark one another – and we need one another to be fellow actors on the stage of Act IV, 'Church'. Communion is not something that happens alone, it requires joining with others.

The current and controversial Windsor Report[35] – addressing the ways in which communion and understanding are enhanced in a situation where serious differences threaten the life of the diverse worldwide Anglican Communion – underlines the importance of the corporate dimension for the interpretation of scripture. It puts it like this:

> As the whole Church, corporately and individually, gives attention to the reading and pondering of scripture, we are called to the specific unifying task of a common *discernment in communion*. We come from a rich variety of cultures, and each of us is called to read scripture within, and apply it to, our own

---

35 Anglican Consultative Council, 2004, London: Anglican Communion Office. For this discussion, see especially paragraphs 67–70, quotation from paragraph 67. Available online at: http://www.anglicancommunion.org/windsor2004/section_b/p7.cfm

particular setting – and to respect the fact that other churches face the same demands within their own contexts. We cannot, therefore, confine our readings of scripture to our own setting alone (as scholarship, sometimes claimed as the preserve of the western academy, has often done). On the contrary, one of the ways in which we discern the limits of appropriate inculturation is by our rendering account to one another, across traditional boundaries, for the gospel we proclaim and live and the teaching we offer. One of the hallmarks of healthy worldwide communion will be precisely our readiness to learn from one another (which by no means indicates an unquestioning acceptance of one another's readings, but rather a rich mutual accountability) as we read scripture together. To the extent that this has not been a major feature of our common life in recent decades, we should not be surprised that major divisions have opened up amongst us. It is by reading scripture too little, not by reading it too much, that we have allowed ourselves to drift apart.

How can a local church contribute to the task of discerning scripture in communion? It is my conviction that the weekly reading of the Old Testament at the eucharist may itself become a challenging but instructive gift for handling diversity and difference. The literature itself speaks with some differing voices – as I have noted, Brueggemann has distinguished three very different kinds of voice among its chapters, corresponding to testimony, dispute and advocacy – which acknowledges the way in which the canon does not look for unity in uniformity but embraces its own lively critique.

The diversity of books in the Bible – especially in the Old Testament – itself invites a diversity of interpreters.[36] For each of us will most likely find different points of resonance, according to our different experiences, personalities and needs. The person who has experienced deep suffering may have particular insight into the book of Job, while the foreigner may relate to the experience of exile as a resident alien. The stories of David misusing power or Solomon executing judgement will be heard differently by rulers and judges than by those who have felt the abuse of power and harsh judgement. Thankfully, the church contains all of these different interpreters – the challenge is to treasure every priceless voice, especially the quieter or more hesitant ones, as its resource for corporate listening.

The way that scripture is read is an important factor in shaping how scripture is heard and shared in a congregation. Church architecture (for example, the position and style of the ambo/lectern) and liturgical choreography (for example, standing and perhaps turning to hear a reading) are symbolic factors that influence our understanding of what is read. So also do dramatic effect and PowerPoint technology, each of which may amplify a text by particular uses of gesture, voice or image. Such techniques are valuable if they enable deep listening and focused reflection – which may include congregational participation and response, formal or

---

36 See further, Samuel Wells, 2006, *God's Companions: Reimagining Christian Ethics*, Oxford: Blackwell.

informal, prescribed or spontaneous. Many churches practise the habit of a period of silence after each reading; others encourage reflection through contemplative music or brief conversation with the person sitting next to them or with the preacher. The measure of the effect of such methods may be discerned through the typical level of expectation prior to the reading (do we eagerly anticipate our imagination to be stretched and shaped?), the concentration during the reading (is the depth of listening and focus infectious?) and the extent to which the reading becomes a part of the conversation during or after the service, whether over coffee or at times in the week beyond. Does the reading enable us to indwell God's word, to live under its authority and within its story?

And does our reading of the Old Testament help build the church – especially when it comes to difference and conflict? It is the Old Testament – to a far greater extent than the New, though relevant there too – that handles issues of unity and diversity. Ambiguity and uncertainty are a gift, not a threat. This is not to say that the Old Testament is uncertain, but rather, it is to say that the Old Testament is not superficial: its multiplicity of meaning enriches rather than problematizes. Isaiah's 'servant' is one key example:[37] Who was he? This is a question unanswered in the text, an open question that has played on Jewish imagination down the ages, with countless candidates proposed ('Is it you? Is it him? Her? Even me?!'). If Christians foreclose the question with the

---

37 See especially Isaiah 53 for the account of the suffering servant; also Isaiah 42, 48, 50 and (arguably) 61.

simple definitive answer – 'Christ' – however 'correct' they may be, they also miss the nuance of the original text, which normally assumed Israel as the servant and which continues to challenge God's people to fulfil that role.

The wondrous depths of the Old Testament are a gift to be plumbed: read, re-read, discussed and enjoyed, but never exhausted. For Christians, special depths unfold as the Old Testament is imagined in relation to the New, with exodus, covenant, passion, resurrection and Pentecost all disclosing the meaning of the different parts of the five-act 'play' of God's presence with God's people. All the while, Hebrew scripture invites Christian readers into God's company with the imperative 'Hallelujah' and the invitation to join the endless praise of angels singing, 'Holy, holy, holy . . .'

Psalms

GORDON MURSELL

Why bother with the Psalms? One answer is because they're there, and more significantly because they come to us with all the immediacy of human experience in the raw, unmediated, not homogenized by sterile church-speak. But they don't just articulate human experience: they explore it, question it, and imagine it differently – and all in the context of worship. In one of the Psalms, a universal problem is explored by the psalmist: the question of why the innocent suffer and the wicked prosper. For the psalmist, this is no academic issue – it threatens to subvert his or her faith:

> my feet were almost gone;
> my steps had well-nigh slipped.
> For I was envious of the proud;
> I saw the wicked in such prosperity. (Psalm 73.2–3)[38]

---

[38] Quotations from the Psalms in this chapter are drawn from *Common Worship*. Sometimes, italics have been added for emphasis by Gordon Mursell.

The psalmist explores this issue at some length, pointing out how the wicked defy God directly by their lifestyle:

They say, 'How should God know?
Is there knowledge in the Most High?' (Psalm 73.11)

So what's the point of being religious (the psalmist asks)? Why believe in God when it does you so little good?

Then thought I to understand this,
but it was too hard for me.
Until I entered the sanctuary of God
and understood the end of the wicked.

(Psalm 73.16–17)

The psalmist prays through this agonizing dilemma, directly confronting its most uncomfortable implications. Then something happens: some gift of perception or understanding is granted, some sense that ultimately evil and those who practise it will not have the last word; and the psalm ends with one of the most intimate experiences of God's presence to be found in the Bible:

Yet I am always with you;
you hold me by my right hand.
You will guide me with your counsel
and afterwards receive me with glory.
Whom have I in heaven but you?
And there is nothing upon earth that I desire
  in comparison with you. (Psalm 73.23–5)

Three things are worth noting here. The first is that, by praying through this question and its intellectual, emotional and spiritual implications, the psalmist does not discover any clear answer: instead, he or she is given precisely what in the first part of the psalm is most at risk – the gift of faith, in a God whose loving purposes will not finally be defeated by evil. Indeed, it is precisely the honest and costly exploration of this question in prayer that leads to the psalmist's renewed and almost childlike sense of God's presence. This seemingly abrupt movement from anguished doubt to an assurance of the divine love should not surprise us; for behind the Psalms lies Israel's belief that God had initiated a covenant between them, the belief that God and Israel together had entered into a lifelong nuptial relationship – and it is precisely this belief that allows the psalmist to bring all of his or her experience of life, including the hard questions, into that relationship: just as the child who believes itself to be unconditionally loved by its parents will similarly feel free to be transparently honest with them, rather than simply have to tell them what they want to hear.[39] It is because of the covenant, because at some deep and corporate level Israel felt it was, or had been, loved and called, that its prayer book, the Psalter, gives expression to almost every conceivable aspect of human experience, from passionate longing and wild celebration to furious anger and envy. And not the least of the reasons why the Psalms must remain central to Christian prayer and worship is because Christians too believe in a God who

---

39 Compare Shakespeare: we should 'speak what we feel, not what we ought to say' (*King Lear*, Act V Scene 3).

loves us unconditionally – and if we don't feel free to share all of our lives with that God, we are not practising, or bearing witness to, what we preach.

Theology, prayer and testimony

The second point to notice in Psalm 73 is that the decisive change takes place *in the sanctuary* (Psalm 73.17). It is there, not in the seminar room or in the solitude of one's home, that the gift of faith, so powerfully under assault from everyday experience of life's randomness and evil, is renewed, and a new experience of God's presence granted. The psalms were written for both personal and corporate prayer, and have been used for both ever since, by Jews and Christians alike. They contain innumerable references to both:

> Come, bless the Lord, all you servants of the Lord,
> you that by night stand in the house of the Lord.
> Lift up your hands *towards the sanctuary*
> and bless the Lord. (Psalm 134.1–2)

> I will give thanks to you, O Lord, with my whole heart;
> before the gods will I sing praise to you.
> I will bow down *towards your holy temple* and praise your name . . .
> (Psalm 138.1–2)

> Now when I think on these things, I pour out my soul:

how I went with the multitude
   and *led the procession to the house of God.*
With the voice of praise and thanksgiving,
among those who kept holy day. (Psalm 42.4–5)

I was glad when they said to me,
'Let us go to the house of the Lord.'
And now our feet are standing
within your gates, O Jerusalem. (Psalm 122.1–2)

O magnify the Lord with me;
let us exalt his name *together*. (Psalm 34.3)

This last quotation brings us to the third point to be noted from our brief exploration of the 73rd Psalm. Like Psalm 34, and many others, Psalm 73 is not all prayer: indeed in the first part of it God is referred to in the third person. This is a crucial and rarely noticed point: in the psalms, theology (talking *about* God) is inseparably connected with prayer (talking *to* God), and both lead to testimony (talking about God to others). Psalm 73 begins with a theological statement that is immediately challenged, and in which God is being talked *about*, not *to*:

Truly, God is loving to Israel,
to those who are pure in heart.
Nevertheless, my feet were almost gone;
my steps had well-nigh slipped.
For I was envious of the proud;
I saw the wicked in such prosperity. (Psalm 73.1–3)

Theology, talk about God, needs to be appropriated, and tested out, in personal experience. Only after this theological exploration, and only on entering the sanctuary, does the psalmist address God directly as 'you':

Until I entered the sanctuary of God
and understood the end of the wicked:
How you set them in slippery places;
you cast them down to destruction. (Psalm 73.17–18)

The psalmist takes his or her theological reflection into the place of worship; and there the movement from theology to prayer is seamless, as is the movement from prayer to testimony in the closing verses:

Truly those who forsake you will perish;
you will put to silence the faithless who betray you.
But it is good for me to draw near to God;
in the Lord God have I made my refuge,
    that I may tell of all your works. (Psalm 73.27–28)

This process happens constantly in the psalms. Sometimes it is the prayer of lament (which in the Bible is, broadly speaking, the way people pray when faith and experience collide painfully with one another) that leads directly, first to testimony . . .

My God, my God, why have you forsaken me;
and are so far from my salvation,
    from the words of my distress? . . .

Save me from the lion's mouth,
   from the horns of wild oxen . . .
I will tell of your name to my people;
in the midst of the congregation will I praise you.
Praise the Lord, you that fear him (Psalm 22.1,
21–23a)

. . . from testimony to liturgy . . .

From you comes my praise in the great congregation;
I will perform my vows
   in the presence of those that fear you (Psalm 22.25)

. . . and from liturgy to theology . . .

For the kingdom is the Lord's
and he rules over the nations. (Psalm 22.28)

Each flows from the other: passionate lament and the unflinching articulation in prayer of the most difficult questions leads the writer or singer of Psalm 22 to a sudden and unexpected assurance that God has not forsaken him or her; and in the end that assurance is given universal scope:

They shall come and make known his salvation,
   to a people yet unborn,
declaring that he, the Lord, has done it. (Psalm 22.31)

So a psalm that begins with the most introspective and narrowly self-centred perspective ('why have you forsaken me?'), rooted in present distress, ends with the most outward-looking and cosmic (we might say evangelistic) perspective ('all the ends of the earth shall remember and turn to the Lord'), rooted in future hope ('they shall come . . .').

This subtle interrelation of theology, prayer and testimony is not restricted to the laments. It appears at its simplest in the most famous psalm of all. The 23rd Psalm begins with moving personal testimony, talking about God to others:

> The Lord is my shepherd;
> therefore can I lack nothing.
> He makes me lie down in green pastures. (Psalm 23.1–2a)

Halfway through, the psalmist shifts from testimony to prayer, addressing God directly:

> Though I walk through the valley of the shadow of death,
>   I will fear no evil;
> for you are with me. (Psalm 23.4)

The prayer continues in a manner that for Christians is eucharistic in tone:

> You spread a table before me
>   in the presence of those who trouble me. (Psalm 23.5a)

The image of God as shepherd (an image that, in the Hebrew Bible, suggests both pastor and ruler, as in the life of David) leads to the image of God as host at table. And this shared meal has a defiant quality – it is celebrated in the face of 'those who trouble me'. Perhaps all true worship should have something of this bold defiance about it: nothing is more infuriating to the powers of evil than when people of faith celebrate their downfall just when they seem to be gaining the upper hand, as Nebuchadnezzar discovered when he was wrongfooted by Shadrach, Meshach and Abed-Nego (see Daniel 3). And the 23rd Psalm ends by returning from worship to testimony, from gratitude to trust, and from present to future:

> Surely goodness and loving mercy shall follow me
>   all the days of my life,
> and I will dwell in the house of the Lord for ever.
> (Psalm 23.6)

The words translated 'goodness' and 'loving mercy' (in Hebrew *tov* and *chesed*) are covenant words, reflecting the loving mutual commitment formalized by God and Israel. The psalmist wants to ponder the nature of that God, celebrate that covenant, and then commend both to others: hence the inseparability of theology, prayer and testimony. In our culture, this is rare: theology is felt to be the domain of university departments, whereas prayer is increasingly felt to be a matter of individual taste and temperament (to be practised in church or in private), while testimony, or evangelism, takes place in the market place or wherever people meet. Furthermore, all three (and certainly the first and the third) are often believed to be best left to experts. Ancient Israel saw no need for such separation, allowing each to inform and enrich the other two, so that good theology makes for good worship and effective evangelism, and all three are rooted in the context of everyday life and of the challenge of trying to live justly in the face of suffering and evil.

Corporate and individual identity

There is something else worth noticing in the texts quoted above: just as the psalms reflect the interrelation of prayer, theology and testimony, so they reflect as well another interrelation – between the individual and the corporate. We have already noticed above how the 22nd Psalm, whose opening verse is recorded by the gospel writers as being prayed by Jesus himself as he hung dying on the cross, moves from what we might call a me-centred to a world-centred perspective. Just as ancient Israel felt much less need than we do to separate study from prayer, or head from heart, so she similarly felt less need to separate the one from the many. 'My God, why have you forsaken me?' can (as we have just suggested) be the voice of a single individual, or of the *persona* of the community or nation. In some psalms, the king fulfils this representative role, speaking for the whole people; hence those prayers for the king (such as Psalm 21), which appear to be unduly sycophantic, can be better read as prayers for national well-being. And in any case, ancient Israel knew better than to put too much trust in those who hold secular power:

> Put not your trust in princes,
>   nor in any human power:
> for there is no help in them. (Psalm 146.2)

> Now therefore be wise, O kings;
> be prudent, you judges of the earth.
> Serve the Lord with fear . . .
> lest he be angry and you perish from the way. (Psalm 2.10–11)

One of the greatest of all interpreters of the psalms, Augustine of Hippo, did more than anyone else to draw attention to the way the individual and the corporate are held together. For him this found supreme expression in his concept of the *totus Christus*, or whole Christ. In his sermon on Psalm 55, Augustine says:

> the body of Christ, the unity of Christ, is crying out in its anguish, its weariness, its affliction, in the distress of its ordeal. It is one single person, a unity grounded in an individual body, and in the distress of its soul it cries from the bounds of the earth: 'from the ends of the earth I have called to you, as my soul grew faint'.[40]

---

[40] Sermon on Psalm 54[55].17, in Augustine, *Expositions on Psalms 52–73*, 2001, *The Works of Saint Augustine*, Part 3 vol. 3, New York: New City Press, translated by Maria Boulding OSB.

Elsewhere Augustine makes the point even more explicitly:

> You can scarcely find any other voice in the psalms than that of Christ and the Church, or of Christ alone, or of the Church alone – the Church which is ourselves, or at any rate of which we form a part. It follows that when we recognize our own voice we can hardly remain unmoved, and our joy is all the more intense as we feel ourselves to be present there.[41]

For Augustine, Christians can never pray a psalm alone: we pray it as members of the body of Christ, the church. In every psalm, the speaker is either Christ himself, as head of the body, or one or more members of the body: the experiences and prayers of individual Christians are drawn into the experiences and prayers of Jesus himself – he prays in us and we in him. So when we read 'my feet were almost gone; my steps had wellnigh slipped' in Psalm 73, we can identify this both with the suffering of the human Christ, and with countless puzzled and stumbling Christians who have sought to follow him, as well as with ourselves and the experience of others known to us. Then Christ prays this with us and through us, and our doubts and brokenness get drawn into the transforming power of his death on the cross. As Augustine puts it, Christ makes his own the attitude even of his enemies, and thereby transforms it.[42]

---

41 Augustine, Sermon on Psalm 59[60].1, in *The Works of Saint Augustine*. The quotation is Psalm 60.3 [61.2].
42 *Hoc in se transfiguravit Dominus*, Sermon on Psalm

Or, as Jason Byassee points out in an excellent study of Augustine on the psalms, Christ takes upon himself our ugliness and sin so that we may share Christ's divine beauty. Nor is this some egocentric process, for the concept of the *totus Christus* is not an end in itself: 'as Christ speaks in both head and members, those members grow in their ability to reflect on the gathering up of all creation in Christ to the Father that is taking place in the liturgy. The chanting of psalms is a central working out of salvation.'[43]

This recognition of the capacity of the psalms to draw us into communion both with God and with one another is crucial, especially for those nurtured in the atomized individualism of European and North American culture. Augustine was African, and the psalms are Middle Eastern: both reflect a culture in which the 'I' and the 'we' are inseparable. In his novel *The Grapes of Wrath*, the great American writer John Steinbeck recognized what happens, especially among the poor and disadvantaged, when the 'I' becomes a 'we':

> One man, one family driven from the land; this rusty car creaking along the highway to the west. I lost my land . . . I am alone and bewildered. And in the night one family camps in a ditch and another family pulls

---

40[41].11, in *Expositions on Psalms 34–51*, 2000, *The Works of Saint Augustine*, Part 3 vol. 2, New York: New City Press, translated by Maria Boulding OSB.

43 Jason Byassee, 2007, *Praise Seeking Understanding: Reading the Psalms with Augustine*, Grand Rapids: Eerdmans, p. 203.

in and the tents come out. Here is the embryo of what [all owners] fear. For here 'I lost my land' is changed; a cell is split and from the splitting grows the thing [they] hate – 'We lost *our* land ... This is the beginning – from 'I' to 'we.' But that you [owners] cannot know. For the quality of owning freezes you for ever into 'I', and cuts you off for ever from the 'we.'[44]

It is this process that the psalms can help to foster. And for Christians it is of course above all in worship that the 'I' can become part of the 'we'. The psalms have been used by Jews and Christians alike in both private and public prayer since they were first written (or rather sung, since it is abundantly clear from the texts themselves that these ancient prayer–poems were designed to be sung, often with musical accompaniment), even though there remains much uncertainty about exactly how and when they were used.[45] In the monasteries,

---

44 John Steinbeck, 1939, *The Grapes of Wrath*, chapter 14.

45 The index to the use of the Psalms appended to Simeon Singer, ed., 1890, The Anglo-Jewish *Authorised Daily Prayer Book*, London (no identified publisher) indicates that 74 out of 150 of the psalms occur in the context of the *Siddur*, or standard daily prayers, the first written texts of which appeared in the ninth century (Stefan C. Reif, 2004, 'The Bible in the Liturgy', Adele Berlin and Marc Zvi Brettler, eds, *The Jewish Study Bible*, Oxford: Oxford University Press, pp. 1938–9). It is possible that the Psalms were used more for personal than for public devotion in the early decades of Christian history: see, for example, Georg P. Braulik, 2004, 'Psalter and Messiah: Towards a Christological Understanding of the Psalms in the Old Testament and the Church Fathers', Dirk J. Human and Cas J. A. Vos, eds, *Psalms and Liturgy*, London: T&T Clark, p. 20, note 16, and Norbert Lohfink, 2003, *In the Shadow of Your Wings: New Readings of*

the entire Psalter was prayed through 'in course', sometimes as often as several times daily; in cathedrals and churches, the history of their use is more complex, but the psalms have always played a central role: from at least the sixth century, a psalm has been sung at the eucharist either as an introit or gradual hymn; in the Roman Catholic, Orthodox and Anglican traditions, they have also retained a fundamental place in the daily office; and in Reformed traditions vernacular translations of the psalms in the form of metrical hymns have ensured them a similarly central role in Sunday services. Nor has their use been confined to worship and private prayer: to give just one example, St Gregory of Nyssa (c.335–94) writes that in his day it was customary for them to be sung at banquets and wedding festivities: 'so that, in these night festivals, by means of these psalms, we are in the presence of enthusiastic hymn singing and the philosophy of the Churches which is enthusiastically pursued in them.'[46]

Ways of praying

Lament

It may be worth concluding by suggesting some of the ways in which the psalms can be used in worship and prayer. Something has already been said about the

---

Great Texts from the Bible, Collegeville: Michael Glazier, especially pp. 76–9.

46 Ronald E. Heine, ed., 1995, Gregory of Nyssa, *Treatise on the Inscriptions of the Psalms*, Oxford: Oxford University Press, p. 88.

psalms of *lament*, and the significance of the covenant as the theological context for this. To feel free to lament, either in public or in private prayer, is to rediscover our status as children of God, and to make our own that childlike boldness which belongs only to those who feel or felt they were unconditionally loved: it is also to bear witness to a God who is not just creator and redeemer but parent and fellow-traveller. Even more important, the freedom to lament, to ask questions in prayer and worship about anything from individual suffering to government policy, is a freedom we take for granted at our peril; for there may come a time when precisely that freedom is no longer to be found in the media or the market place, as Walter Brueggemann has memorably pointed out.[47] We can pray these great psalms for those who are today sharing in the suffering described by the psalmist, thereby giving a voice to those who have no voice: the 55th Psalm makes a powerful prayer for a victim of rape, the 59th for a victim of urban vio-

---

47 'A community of faith which negates laments soon concludes that the hard issues of justice are improper questions to pose at the throne [of God], because the throne seems to be only a place of praise. I believe it thus follows that if justice questions are improper questions at the throne (which is a conclusion drawn through liturgic use), they soon appear to be improper questions in public places, in schools, in hospitals, with the government, and eventually even in the courts. Justice questions disappear into civility and docility. The order of the day comes to seem absolute, beyond question, and we are left with only grim obedience and eventually despair. The point of access for serious change has been forfeited when the propriety of this speech form is denied' (Walter Brueggemann, 1986, 'The Costly Loss of Lament', *Journal for the Study of the Old Testament* 36, pp. 57–71, p. 64).

lence, the 44th for a community who feel abandoned by God and everyone else, the 88th for someone living with AIDS.

Praise

The childlike, covenantal nature of lament is what leads to the close relationship between lament and intimacy in such texts as Psalm 73, as we have already seen. Equally important is the close relationship between lament and *praise*: many (though not all) of the great laments move from past or present to future, from the individual's experience to the life of the whole people of God, and from lament to praise.[48] And in the psalms praise is not the same as thanksgiving: rather it is an active and hopeful envisioning of a new and different future that often emerges precisely out of experiences of lament and exile, of people praying where they are not in control and not where they want to be. Even when it appears on its own, praise in the psalms almost invariably invites those praying to enlarge their horizons. It is the best possible corrective to a narrow introspection or dull churchiness. Consider the way these three prayers invite us to look forward, first to the day when all people praise our God:

O praise the Lord, all you nations:
praise him, *all you peoples*. (Psalm 117.1)

---

48 The Hebrew word for the Psalms is *Tehilim*, 'Songs of Praise'.

The last psalm in the Psalter goes further, inviting creatures to join in:

Let *everything that has breath*
praise the Lord. (Psalm 150.6)

But the 100th Psalm dreams of a day when even the humblest parts of creation participate in cosmic praise:

O be joyful in the Lord, *all the earth*;
serve the Lord with gladness
   and come before his presence with a song. (Psalm 100.1)

Dreaming of a day when stones as well as zebras praise God with us may be wishful thinking on the psalmist's part. But we might do well to recall that it was wishful thinking – in the strict sense of pondering the possibility of dreams coming true – that led to many of the most crucial changes in life and society during human history. Furthermore, inviting the non-human creation to share our praise of God is an invitation to the best kind of eco-friendly spirituality, in which the earth shares our travails and will one day be set free with us from harm and decay. The imagery of the Psalter is drawn almost entirely from the created world, often from its wildest and least tamed aspects: the people of God (and God too) are like mountains (Psalm 125.1–2), abusers of power are like deaf snakes (Psalm 58.4), the victim of evil or suffering like 'an owl that haunts the ruins' or 'a sparrow, solitary upon the housetop' (Psalm 102.7–8) – and so on.

Confession

The psalms also contain some profound and searching material for prayers of *confession*. The 51st Psalm begins:

> Have mercy on me O God in your great goodness:
> according to the abundance of your compassion blot out my offences.
> Wash me thoroughly from my wickedness:
> and cleanse me from my sin. (Psalm 51.1–2)

Here, the full appalling reality of sin is held together with the fullness of God's mercy: the Hebrew word *rachamim*, here translated 'fullness of compassion', derives from a noun meaning 'womb' and denotes God's womb-like, maternal love for the sinner. Sin is here described both as law-breaking (Psalm 51.1b), an objective state of distortion of alienation from reality (Psalm 51.2a), a losing of our way on our spiritual journeys (Psalm 51.2b), and a state of radical rebellion against God (Psalm 51.3a). For this psalmist, it has the character of a cancerous growth: once allowed to obtain a foothold in our lives, it acquires a terrible energy and momentum of its own, and will if unchecked end up destroying us. This is the force of the psalmist's unflinching honesty about its origins:

> I have been wicked even from my birth,
> a sinner when my mother conceived me. (Psalm 51.6)

This is not a general statement about humanity, or a theological reflection about original sin. Rather it is the specific acknowledgment of a personal sin whose roots lie deep in the origins of my own being. No one expresses this point more clearly than John Donne, in his sermon on this psalm: 'You must not reckon in sin, from the Nativity, but from the Conception; when you conceived that sin in your purpose, then you sinned that sin.'[49] He goes on to say that 'sins which are but the children of indifferent actions, become the Parents of great sins.' But what is really remarkable in this psalm is the way in which both human sin and divine mercy are taken with ultimate seriousness: just as the former can and does infect the whole cosmos, so the latter can use even our most appalling failures as the seedbed for a new society.

Resources for the journey

There is space to mention just one other aspect of the psalms: their capacity to serve as what we might call rucksack prayer,[50] spiritual resources we can carry with us on our journeys through life. The psalms may well have been designed to be learnt by heart, and their astonishingly varied use of images both earths their concerns

---

49 G. R. Potter and E. M. Simpson, eds, 1953–62, *The Sermons of John Donne*, Berkeley: California University Press, vol. 5, p. 15.

50 For the idea of a spiritual 'knapsack', see Alan Wilkinson and Christopher Cocksworth, eds, 1996, *An Anglican Companion: Words from the Heart of Faith*, London: Church House Publishing.

and enables them to lodge in the memory in a way few other prayers can do. One psalm above all others needs mentioning here, and it is the longest and least understood of them all. The 119th Psalm may be the prayer of a scribe, or (surely more likely) of an exiled Jew in Babylon, deprived of synagogue and home but able to hold in both heart and mind the lifegiving power of the *torah*, God's providential guidance and wisdom for daily living:

> I am a stranger upon earth;
> hide not your commandments from me. (Psalm 119.19)

The word translated 'stranger' is the Hebrew *ger*, meaning 'sojourner' or 'resident alien'. This is the prayer of someone uprooted from where they belong, yet who draws on shared memories and wisdom, a portable sanctuary or spiritual rucksack that can be carried into places of exile and pain, and through these a faith to renew his or her sense of a God who is a fellow-nomad. That faith makes the psalmist defiant:

> I will tell of your testimonies, even before kings,
> and will not be ashamed. (Psalm 119.46)

And it allows him or her to allow that defiance to collide with present experiences of a barren, dried-out loneliness:

> I have become like a wineskin in the smoke,
> yet I do not forget your statutes. (Psalm 119.83)

Throughout, the imagery is of a journey — references to ways, roads, travelling and pilgrimage abound; and the way travelled is hazardous:

The proud have dug pits for me
in defiance of your law. (Psalm 119.85)

But the overwhelmingly central theme is that of *torah*: the many synonyms used in English translations (law, statutes, commandments and so on) do scant justice to the Hebrew originals, and can cause us to give up after a few verses and miss the main point, not just of this wonderful psalm but of the entire Psalter. At the heart of Psalm 119 are three primary realities: the self (which can, as we have seen, stand for the whole community), God, and God's word. It bears witness to a God who speaks, and who longs to be spoken to in response. And the word of God, as we read it in both Old and New Testaments, is a word both of comfort and of judgement, of instruction and hope. Spirituality and ethics, prayer and just living, cannot be separated; and for Christians, for whom the word was made flesh and dwelt among us, the 'commandment' becomes the divine made human, the love of God with an infinite power to change our lives:

I have seen an end of all perfection,
but your commandment knows no bounds. (Psalm 119.96)

New Testament

JOY TETLEY

Christian scriptures in the eucharist

Without the New Testament, there would be no eucharist. Such a bold (and bald) assertion looks beyond the New Testament as a collection of writings to the transformative reality those writings express and explore. Both sacred texts and sacramental actions celebrate and communicate the blessings and challenges of the new covenant, sealed in the body and blood of Jesus Christ. The words 'testament' and 'covenant' are, indeed, interchangeable, as the Prayer of Consecration in *The Book of Common Prayer* neatly illustrates:

> Likewise after supper he took the Cup; and when he had given thanks, he gave it to them saying, Drink ye all of this; for this is my Blood of the New Testament, which is shed for you and for many for the remission of sins: Do this, as oft as ye shall drink it, in remembrance of me.

The eucharist is the sacrament of that new covenant to which the New Testament texts bear witness. Those texts make a vital contribution to the liturgy, whatever precise form it may take, whether in terms of defined readings or through their suffusion of the whole service. The eucharistic liturgy is shot through with scriptural phraseology and allusion, not least from the New Testament. The more our eyes are opened to this interweaving, the richer the pattern becomes, and the deeper its meaning.

The eucharist invites us to encounter, to meeting, to communion. It is the church's focal opportunity to realize her privileged vocation as the Body of Christ, both in the sense of recognition and of incarnation. Participating together in the liturgy, the people of God, if they will, can begin to perceive the truth of who they really are and to give flesh to that reality. Corporately and individually, they partake in and of Christ's life. They also bear the awesome responsibility of living out in the world Christ's saving presence and love. Crucially, whether they like it or not, that requires them to acknowledge the presence of Christ in one another. Encountering the living God is, so to speak, horizontal as well as vertical. Participating in Christ's life and mission cannot be confined to the pursuit of private communion. Still less should it co-exist with the rejection or condemnation of sisters and brothers in Christ.

Making connections: the eucharist and Hebrews

In the context of 'approaching the throne of grace', the author of the letter to the Hebrews makes this point with typical pastoral sharpness: 'And let us consider how to provoke one another to love and good deeds, not neglecting to meet together, as is the habit of some, but encouraging one another . . .' (Hebrews 10.24, 25). If God's people are to be provocative, it must be for positive, Christ-like reasons – after the manner of Christ himself – so that the world may believe and enjoy God's blessing (compare John 17).

The New Testament texts leave us in no doubt that God's new covenant, celebrated in the eucharist, brings responsibility as well as privilege. It is a mercy, then, that at the heart of this new covenant lies forgiveness. Among all the New Testament writings, it is the letter to the Hebrews that treats most extensively and explicitly of the new covenant's significance in Christian faith and life. It repays some focused attention, therefore. It may also serve as a telling example of how engaging with sacred scripture (not least in the context of worship) may propel us into engagement with the living God. In and through and beyond the contextuality and human instrumentality of the written word, the voice of God still resonates. And it still both comforts and confronts.

Hebrews is an intriguing, adventurous and powerful work. We do not know who produced it, nor the precise location and identity of those who first received it. Yet its message takes us into the depths of God and challenges us to become who we were meant to be, in the mercy and grace of Christ. The author of Hebrews is essentially a preacher, on fire with God and with pastoral concern for a community in crisis. For reasons that are not spelt out, that community is seriously discouraged, falling apart and tempted to give up on allegiance to Jesus. What they receive from their concerned but absent pastor-figure is not a dispassionate academic treatise but an urgent exhortation, which is yet carefully structured and carefully argued. With equal passion, both mind and heart are engaged. The language and imagery used relate primarily to Jewish scripture and experience, probably reflecting the background of both author and receiving community. The message that language carries, if not the religious context it inhabits, is readily accessible, at all times and in all places, for it has to do with the very accessibility of God.

Indeed, the privilege of direct access to God is a central feature of what the author is trying to get across, in order to put fresh heart into this ailing and failing community and keep them on the way of Christ. So his sermon is permeated with the theme and ethos of worship (and in all probability, like much of the rest of the New Testament material, it was designed to be read out to a congregation assembled for worship). It is perhaps not surprising, therefore, that although Hebrews has been comparatively neglected in terms of academic study and, perhaps, personal devotion, it has nonetheless contributed significantly over the centuries to liturgy and hymnody, thereby slipping unawares under many a Christian skin. That is also true, of course, of a good many other New Testament texts. It can be a worthwhile exercise to pursue and ponder those connections.

In terms of Hebrews it may suffice, by way of example, to point to some of the influence it has exerted on liturgical material to be found in *Common Worship: Services and Prayers for the Church of England* (2000). Taking

Holy Communion Order 1, we find a number of major associations. First, there is the Prayer of Preparation:

> Almighty God,
> to whom all hearts are open,
> all desires known,
> and from whom no secrets are hidden:
> cleanse the thoughts of our hearts
> by the inspiration of your Holy Spirit,
> that we may perfectly love you,
> and worthily magnify your holy name;
> through Christ our Lord.

This ancient prayer, used liturgically for many centuries, is generally attributed to St Gregory, Abbot of Canterbury in the late eighth century AD. It carries great spiritual power, and if prayed at all seriously, brings home the fearful reality of our condition before God. Nothing can be hidden and there is nowhere to hide – a salutary reminder as we draw near to God in worship and one that fittingly propels us into the Prayers of Penitence. This Collect for Purity (as it is more traditionally known) is heavy with scriptural insight and allusion. Psalm 51 certainly echoes loudly through it. And so does a seminal passage from Hebrews:

> Indeed, the word of God is living and active, sharper than any two-edged sword, piercing until it divides soul from spirit, joints from marrow; it is able to judge the thoughts and intentions of the heart. And before God no creature is hidden, but all are naked and laid

bare to the eyes of the one to whom we must render our account. (Hebrews 4.12–13)

Total exposure before God is a terrifying truth. It thus matters, crucially, what God is like. What transforms terror into salvation is the conviction to which Hebrews gives focal attention, i.e. that the 'character' of God is to be perceived and experienced in Jesus. So the preacher immediately follows this stark reminder of utter vulnerability (which almost certainly refers back to the narrative of Adam and Eve's fall in the Garden of Eden) with *good* news:

> Since, then, we have a great high priest who has passed through the heavens, Jesus, the Son of God, let us hold fast to our confession. For we do not have a high priest who is unable to sympathize with our weaknesses, but we have one who in every respect has been tested as we are, yet without sin. Let us therefore approach the throne of grace with boldness, so that we may receive mercy and find grace to help in time of need. (Hebrews 4.14–16)

Our nakedness before God should not prompt us to run away, vainly in search of some protective covering (and that attempt can, of course, take many forms). Rather, we should move boldly and confidently in God's direction. There is no need for escapism or, indeed, grovelling. If we are laid bare before God, then, in Jesus, God is laid bare before us. What we find, therefore, is profound empathy, mercy and grace. God knows. The true meaning of that expletive cries out from God's heart. That, urges Hebrews, should bring much-needed encouragement, in every sense of the word. We can and must 'draw near', not fearful but confident, acknowledging the truth of our condition, yet assured of a knowing welcome that can make us better.

It will be noted that to help bring home this message, Hebrews presents Jesus as 'great high priest'. It is a perception of some importance in this homiletic epistle, and one that in terms of explicit reference and scope of treatment is unique to Hebrews in the New Testament canon. Yet it is a picture which has captured the attention and imagination of many subsequent Christian thinkers and liturgists. That remains true if we return to Common Worship and our sample eucharistic liturgy. So, one of the set invitations to confession picks up on the passage quoted above from Hebrews 4, along with a related text from Hebrews 10.21–22:

> Seeing we have a great high priest who has passed into the heavens,
> Jesus, the Son of God,
> let us draw near with a true heart,
> in full assurance of faith,
> and make our confession to our heavenly Father.

Some of the eucharistic prayers make significant use of this imagery. Thus, for example, eucharistic prayer A:

> Therefore, heavenly Father,
> we remember his offering of himself

> made once for all upon the cross . . .
> Accept through him, our great high priest,
> this our sacrifice of thanks and praise.

and eucharistic prayer B:

> his perfect sacrifice made once for the sins of the whole world . . .
> as we offer you this our sacrifice of praise and thanksgiving . . .

Eucharistic prayer C reads in part:

> For he is our great high priest . . .
> who made there by his one oblation of himself once offered
> a full, perfect and sufficient sacrifice, oblation and sacrifice
> for the sins of the whole world . . .
> Therefore, Lord and heavenly Father. . .
> we offer you through him this our sacrifice of praise and thanksgiving . . .

Other examples include the extended preface for Ascension Day to Pentecost and the extended preface for the Reign of Christ: 'For he is our great high priest who has entered once for all into the heavenly sanctuary . . .'; 'For with the oil of gladness you have anointed Christ the Lord, your only Son, to be our great high priest and king of all creation. As priest he offered himself once for all upon the altar of the cross and redeemed the human race by this perfect sacrifice of peace. As king he claims dominion over all your creatures . . .'

Jesus as high priest

The above examples connect with further dimensions of Hebrews' vision of Jesus as high priest. In the cultural understanding of the community addressed by Hebrews, priesthood was intimately associated with the offering of sacrifice. In Jewish tradition, the priests were responsible for an extensive ritual system, which sought to enable safe access to and communication with a holy God. This system (see especially the book of Leviticus) was seen as God's gracious provision – a way of dealing with human sin and uncleanness. Sacrifice had a central role. One of prime and focal significance was made on the annual Day of Atonement (see Leviticus 16). On this day, the high priest (and he alone) went into the Holy of Holies, the innermost sanctuary where God was believed specially to dwell. On behalf of all the people, he offered the blood of the animal sacrifice, praying that by that offering, with the repentance it betokened, God would set aside the people's sins. It was a sacrifice that had to be repeated year after year by a high priest who, despite all the rites of purification he went through, remained a sinful human being. He was also, like all his fellow priests, from a particular dynastic tribe. Only those of the tribe of Aaron could be priests (Leviticus 8). In effect, being a priest depended on being born into the right family.

Hebrews argues powerfully that this dispensation

has come to an end, because what it was feeling after has been brought to fulfilment, by God's initiative and God's doing. It is absolutely fitting to see Jesus as high priest because Jesus has opened up a 'new and living way' into God's very presence, making fully possible that holy communion with a holy God, which the traditional priesthood was designed to facilitate. For the priesthood of Jesus is the fleshing out of God's own priestly character – God's determined yearning that all should know God, all should have free and confident access into the divine presence, all should share the divine life. Jesus the Son of God is none other than 'radiance of God's glory and exact imprint of God's very being' (Hebrews 1.3). Therefore, 'looking to Jesus' means seeing into the life of God.

Jesus expresses God's longing and commitment to meet us where we are and lead us into glory. That meant, for God in Jesus, sharing fully in human experience and going through incalculable suffering, to the extent of offering up his own life. It also meant bursting out of the boundaries of existing Jewish understandings of priesthood. Here is a God who does not always fit in with traditions and expectations. Jesus did not come from the right tribe to be a priest (Hebrews 7.13, 14). He is perceived, therefore, as priest 'after the order of Melchizedek', that mysterious outsider, on the margins of sacred history. God does a new thing. Indeed, there has to be a change in the law (Hebrews 7.12) to accommodate this change in God's *modus operandi*. Tradition has to be seen in a new light because God has been revealed in a clearer light. Yet behind what might seem like a radical break with the past lies fundamental continuity – the unchanging faithfulness of the God whose mission (whatever the cost) is the realization of blessing and communion, embracing no less than the whole creation (see especially Hebrews 2).

The discouraged community addressed by Hebrews would undoubtedly have found this a challenging message to digest (cf. Hebrews 5.11—6.3) but it was designed to give them a new lease of life and a more mature understanding. So also with those who come after. Seeing Jesus as great high priest uncovers the presence of God, breaking down all barriers, of whatever kind, thereby giving direct access into the holiest of territory. This is most certainly cause for rejoicing. But it can also be hard to take advantage of. Barriers, in fact, can make us feel safer. The prospect of facing up to God for ourselves can engender a sense of threat as well as promise. For it means that we have to take full responsibility. And who knows what God might ask of us? Sending intermediaries might, after all, keep us at a safe, more comfortable distance. Yet that, as Hebrews reminds us in uncompromising fashion, would be to throw away the most life-transforming opportunity there could ever be. Draw near, urges Hebrews; draw near to the throne of grace and discover this truth for yourselves.

Through the priestly initiative of God in Jesus, God and humankind are brought together for good. The 'shadows' of the former things give way to the real thing (Hebrews 10.1). 'Types and shadows have their ending', as the eucharistic hymn puts it. And, surprisingly, it is sometimes the most 'shadowy' of shadows which point to the most searching illumination. The figure of Melchizedek was part of the tradition, but hardly mainstream. It is from this tangential obscurity, however, that a priest 'after his order' (though yet unique) brings 'great salvation' (see especially Hebrews 7). The 'former things', godly though their provenance and purpose may have been, cannot confine or define God. The only constraint upon God is that of absolute, divine love.

Such love led to the death of Jesus 'outside the camp' (Hebrews 13.11, 12), outside the boundaries of religious acceptability. As Hebrews sees it, it is an unqualified priest who offers the ultimate sacrifice. The priests of Aaron's line offered animal sacrifices. In Jesus, God offers his own life, for us and to us. Nothing more is needed. The only sacrifices that continue to be appropriate are sacrifices of praise and generosity (Hebrews 13.15, 16). Though these can be demanding enough, they are but a response to the indescribable outpouring of grace in the shedding of Christ's blood.

Jesus, then, is both priest and victim. There can be no other priesthood to match this. This is the 'end' of priesthood – the perfect fulfilment of priestly ministry. What he accomplished was 'once for all'. It cannot be repeated or bettered, though as a much-sung communion hymn, drawing heavily on Hebrews, puts it:

what he never can repeat
he shows forth day by day.

Of this divine priesthood, all can taste the fruits. And though it cannot be emulated, all are invited to participate in its outworking in the life of the world. As Hebrews says, 'we have become partners of Christ' (Hebrews 3.14). The First Letter of Peter spells it out more fully: 'you are ... a royal priesthood ... in order that you may proclaim the mighty acts of the one who called you out of darkness into the marvellous light of God' (1 Peter 2.9). God's people are called to share in God's priestly mission, that all may find their flourishing in communion with the giver of light and life. This may not always be an easy or happy experience, something that our spiritual forebears in the Hebrews community clearly needed to learn. 'Let us then go to him outside the camp and bear the abuse he endured' (Hebrews 13.13). In God's passion for the world, pain and joy are inseparably linked. Such is the consequence of unbounded love.

Within this calling of the people of God, there will be many and various particular expressions, the ordained priesthood/presbyterate among them. But the presiding minister at the eucharist is no substitute for that great high priest, through whom we draw near to the throne of grace. Those authorized to preside at the Lord's table have a vital role in enabling God's people to celebrate the feast. But they do so as fellow participants in the body and blood of Christ, both sacramentally and in terms of mission and ministry. They have the responsibility and privilege of being servant leaders: servants of the Servant and servants of the servants of God.

Hebrews' insight into Jesus as great high priest is indeed rich with blessing and challenge. When we encounter this imagery in a eucharistic context, however, it can so easily be neutered of its truly startling character by liturgical familiarity. That perhaps points up the need for a raising of awareness of the crucial connection between liturgy and scripture, even beyond the set readings. Sermons are certainly a major opportunity to engage with this, but more is needed in terms of exploration and study outside the formal constraints of a service. Otherwise, in every sense, so much potential for communion is missed.

Fulfilment of divine promise

As 'communion' is at the heart of God's priestly character, so is it at the heart of God's new covenant. Indeed, as Hebrews makes clear, the two are inextricably related. By the offering of himself, Jesus our great high priest inaugurates the new covenant and seals it with his own blood. We are strongly reminded of this by the benediction at the end of Hebrews, which is taken up as the Eastertide blessing in the *Common Worship* resources:

> The God of peace,
> who brought again from the dead our Lord Jesus,
> that great shepherd of the sheep,
> through the blood of the eternal covenant,
> make you perfect in every good work to do his will,
> working in you that which is well-pleasing in his
>   sight;
> and the blessing of God Almighty,
> the Father, the Son and the Holy Spirit,
> be among you and remain with you always.[51]

---

51 See *Common Worship*, Seasonal Resources, p. 317.

By this stage in the service (as by this stage in Hebrews) there should be no doubt of the enormity of the significance of this covenant relationship. It has been highlighted, focally, during the words of institution:

> In the same way, after supper
> he took the cup and gave you thanks;
> he gave it to them, saying:
> Drink this, all of you;
> this is my blood of the new covenant,
> which is shed for you and for many for the
>   forgiveness of sins.
> Do this, as often as you drink it,
> in remembrance of me.

In the same night that he was betrayed, on the eve of the greatest crisis in his life, Jesus provides his followers with the wherewithal both to begin to interpret his death and (even more profoundly) to enter into the sacred mystery of his body and blood – the sacrament of the new covenant.

As Hebrews makes clear (more so than any other New Testament writer) this new covenant is the fulfilment of the divine promise made through the prophecy of Jeremiah:

> The days are surely coming, says the LORD, when I will make a new covenant with the house of Israel and the house of Judah. It will not be like the covenant that I made with their ancestors, on the day when I took them by the hand to lead them out of the land of Egypt

– a covenant that they broke, though I was married to them, says the LORD. But this is the covenant that I shall make with the house of Israel after those days, says the LORD: I will put my law within them, and write it on their hearts; and I will be their God, and they shall be my people. No longer shall they teach one another, or say to each other, 'Know the LORD', for they shall all know me, from the least of them to the greatest, says the LORD; for I will forgive their iniquity, and I will remember their sin no more. (Jeremiah 31.31–34, which is quoted in Hebrews 8.8–12)

A committed relationship that will last forever

As beneficiaries of this covenant, it is incumbent on all the followers of Jesus to ponder its nature and engage with its implications. The first thing to note is that the new covenant is entirely of God's initiative and of God's making (notice the number of first-person-singular pronouns in the prophecy). That is also the case with the other significant examples of covenant recorded in scripture: that involving the whole of creation after the great Flood (Genesis 9.8–17); that with Abraham, involving the promise of descendants and the land (Genesis 15); the Sinai covenant, with Moses and the liberated people of God in the wilderness (Exodus 24) and the covenant with King David, fulfilled in 'great David's greater Son' (2 Samuel 7; Psalm 89). God, it seems, is given to reaching out with binding commitment; and to the benefit, not only of the immediate recipients but, through them, to the benefit of all that God has made.

It is of no little importance, also, that God tends to make covenant at times of crisis, despair and bewilderment in the experience of those, as it were, on the receiving end: after the devastation of the Flood; at a time when Abraham was in despair of the feasibility of God's promise of offspring; at a time when the people of God were wandering, lost and unfaithful, in the wilderness. And true to the divine character, the prophecy of a new covenant comes when God's people have been through the shattering trauma of comprehensive defeat and destruction, provoking a faith and identity crisis of the highest order. God's new promise came when all seemed lost. It was fulfilled, on a dark Friday, when all seemed lost. Its message of hope was proclaimed in Hebrews to a community lost on the way. It still speaks, at all times and in all places, not least when the context seems devoid of promise.

What, then, does it betoken, this new covenant celebrated and communicated in the eucharist? It is fundamentally about God's offer of a committed relationship that will last for ever. It is the guarantee of God's faithfulness, mercy and grace. It holds out, to all who will take it, the deepest forgiveness possible – and the astounding assurance that God forgets as well as forgives ('I will remember their sin no more'). It invites God's people to relate to God with the whole of their lives, not least with their 'hearts'. In biblical imagery, this is not so much the seat of the emotions as the seat of the will, the very core of being. If God's laws are put into our hearts, then the very set of our lives will be towards God and God's values, however we may 'feel' about it. Those values are discovered and explored by 'looking to Jesus', not primarily through detached and distanced study (though this may well be an important facet of it) but directly, at the throne of grace, through a relationship of 'knowing'. 'They shall all know me.' In biblical usage and understanding, 'knowing' has most to do with the intimacy of close relationship (it is often used of sexual intercourse). Knowing God in this way is about communing with God and, therefore, as St Paul puts it in 1 Corinthians 13, 'being known'. Indeed, there is the rub. Working towards abstract knowledge is safer. This kind of knowing relationship involves, on both sides, the risk of handing over at a deep level. Yet, as we have seen, such mutual exposure is entirely in the interests of blessing and communion.

Blessing and communion for *all*, 'from the least of them to the greatest'. God's new covenant commitment is fully comprehensive, both in motivation and scope. Direct access into God's presence is open to all who will come, whatever their background or status. It needs only the briefest of glances at the ministry of Jesus, as recorded in the gospels, to underscore that transforming truth. There, in fact, it is often the most unlikely characters who recognize and respond to Christ's gracious invitation and challenge. Around the table of the Lord, there is still a rich diversity of companionship to be enjoyed.

Nor is that limited by space and time. In the eucharist, through our communion with Christ, we are in communion with those who participate in the body and blood of Christ throughout the world. As St Paul put it (in a phrase often taken up in later liturgy), 'we who are many are one body, for we all partake of the one bread' (1 Corinthians 10.17). In worship, we are also one with that 'great multitude that no one could count' in the glory of heaven (Revelation 7.9). The author of Hebrews is in no doubt about that. In language that resonates through the liturgies and hymnody of the ages, the preacher seeks to encourage a flagging community by reminding them:

> You have come to Mount Zion and to the city of the living God, the heavenly Jerusalem, and to innumerable angels in festal gathering, and to the assembly of the firstborn who are enrolled in heaven, and to God the judge of all, and to the spirits of the righteous made perfect, and to Jesus, the mediator of a new covenant, and to the sprinkled blood that speaks a better word than the blood of Abel. (Hebrews 12.22–24)

The *Common Worship* Invitation to Confession on All Saints' Day takes up another passage in Hebrews which highlights the same theme, again painting a vivid verbal picture:

> Since we are surrounded by a great cloud of witnesses, let us also lay aside every weight and the sin that clings so closely, looking to Jesus in penitence and faith. (cf. Hebrews 12.1, 2)

What is visible by no means defines the fullness of the eucharistic reality. There is so much more.

A gospel to proclaim

Those who benefit from participation in the sacrament of the new covenant thus have a gospel to proclaim. In a very significant sense, they do so by the very act of participating. As St Paul put it to the Corinthian Christians, 'as often as you eat this bread and drink the cup, you proclaim the Lord's death until he comes' (1 Corinthians. 11.26). It does not end there, however. Receiving the life of Christ in this way carries the covenant imperative of living out that life in the world – of being carriers of the good news of God, 'infecting' others with God's blessing.

A major resource in the context of the eucharist for understanding what this might involve is supplied by the set readings from scripture. The epistles can be particularly significant in this regard, as they were written for early Christian communities grappling with how they should live as God's new covenant people (and often, clearly, not making the best job of it). The advice and exhortation proffered by those who wrote to them has the capacity to speak directly to us now, cutting through the boundaries of time and culture. For it is fundamentally about relationship: in and among the members of Christ's church, with the wider human community and, indeed, with the whole of God's creation.

We may consider the following, for instance, from our exemplar text of Hebrews:

> Pursue peace with everyone . . . See to it that no one fails to obtain the grace of God; that no root of bitter-

ness springs up and causes trouble, and through it many become defiled . . . Let mutual love continue. Do not neglect to show hospitality to strangers, for by doing that some have entertained angels without knowing it. Remember those who are in prison, as though you were in prison with them; those who are being tortured, as though you yourselves were being tortured. Let marriage be held in honour by all . . . Keep your lives free from the love of money . . . Do not neglect to do good and to share what you have, for such sacrifices are pleasing to God. (Hebrews 12.14, 15; 13.1–5, 16)

The community addressed here were, of course, in a very different place from us. But the exhortations they receive need very little cultural translation. They still speak, and they still challenge. They are still (in words used in the English coronation service to describe the scriptures as a whole) 'the lively oracles of God'. The texts we know collectively as the New Testament (like all the biblical writings) were born out of experience: out of faith and doubt; out of celebration and struggle; out of joy and anguish. They are prompted by particular, often compelling situations and coloured in their expression by their culture, religious background and context. But they are nonetheless recognizable. All human life is there. And all human life in all shades of relationship with a God who both comforts and confronts. In these ancient documents from a faraway world, we can still come face to face with ourselves and with the living God. And it can be a liberation to discover that, through the Bible, we can find *our* story in *God's* story, our story in the story of God's people of old.

Excited by the Bible readings?

But how are these connections to be realized? On a very practical level (but one that can too often be neglected) the readings need to be delivered in a way that is both audible and articulate, expressive of the lively communications they were meant to be. Those kind enough to 'read the lessons' can only benefit themselves and others if they are appropriately encouraged and enabled to learn more about what they are reading and how they might more effectively get it across. It is also vital, of course, that those on the receiving end are motivated to listen with quality attention, expectant and open to the messages of God. If God's people are to be excited, rather than bored or baffled by the Bible readings, then the church needs to take its task of education seriously.

Within the setting of the eucharist itself, a significant opportunity for that comes with the 'sermon slot'. Here, in a fitting manner, the readings can (to some extent, at least) be explored and interpreted. To use a paradigm persuasively expounded by Frances Young, the biblical material constitutes a richly varied classic repertoire that needs to be skilfully 'performed' if we are to hear and appreciate its music.[52] In this sense, the preacher is a primary instrument in performing the text. And, as Profes-

---

[52] Frances Young, 1990, *The Art of Performance: Towards a Theology of Holy Scripture*, London: Darton, Longman & Todd.

sor Young puts it, this 'is not just a matter of acquiring technical skill, nor just a matter of skills in communication and in projecting personality. The inspired "musicality" of the performer has to be fostered by bringing the old score and present experience into creative interaction'.[53] Whatever methodological approach the preacher might employ, biblical preaching matters. The church cries out for such 'music'. So does the world for which Christ died.

And that brings us back to the heart of the matter. The scriptures, as a whole, bear witness to the God of covenant faithfulness. The New Testament bears specific testimony to the fulfilment of God's promised new covenant in and through Jesus Christ. In the eucharist, whose liturgy is shot through with scriptural language and imagery, we encounter this God; the God whose presence and commitment breathes through the biblical texts, enlivening them and giving them godly meaning, yet never confined or controlled by them. This God will never be trapped in the form of words, however holy. Yet, as fruit of unimaginable divine humility and love, God's life is willingly broken open and offered, once for all, to and for all, that offering profoundly signified in sacramental communion. The invitation to draw near, to allow ourselves to receive the blessings of the new covenant, betokens the offer of a special relationship that is yet meant to bring transformative blessing to all.

Here, indeed, is sacred mystery. The challenge is to entrust ourselves to it.

---

53 Young, *Art of Performance*, p. 162.

Gospels

ANDREW GREGORY

Starting with the Emmaus encounter

It was only after Jesus had interpreted to them the scriptures that the disciples on the Emmaus road recognized him in the breaking of the bread. Just as the reading and application of God's word may prepare its hearers to meet with Jesus at his table, so that encounter makes most sense when understood in the light of the story found in scripture. That is the theological claim that I hope to discuss and defend in what follows.

This chapter is in four main parts. It begins with a brief overview in which I look at the important role played by the gospels both in the Liturgy of the Word and the Liturgy of the Sacrament, the two parts into which contemporary western eucharists are usually divided. I then look, second, at the four gospels that we read, and the three-year cycle according to which we read them. This leads, third, to the nature of the relationship between the gospels and to the other readings that precede them, and questions that arise from the dominance of the gospels in the lectionary. Finally, fourth, and most important, I try to let the gospels speak for themselves. Here we see how scripture may be read and heard in the eucharist as God's word to God's people, those whom Jesus invites to gather round his table and to eat and to drink his body and his blood.

Reading the gospels in the eucharist

That the reading of one of the gospels plays an important role in the celebration of the eucharist should come as no surprise to anyone who worships in an Anglican church, or in other Christian traditions. Worshippers often stand when the gospel is read, and in many churches the book that contains the gospel reading is carried formally into the church at the beginning of the service, and into the middle of the congregation before its content is proclaimed.[54] These are clear visual indications of the centrality of the gospels in the eucharist, but there are also less visible but no less significant ways in which the communion service makes clear the importance of the gospels and their witness to Jesus.

This is true both of the first part of the service (usually referred to as the Liturgy of the Word) and of the second (usually referred to as the Liturgy of the Sacrament). Not only does the gospel come as the last and climactic

---

[54] Other ceremonial elements may also be present. These include the reader of the gospel preparing to read by seeking the blessing of the presider, or the reader kissing the gospel book. In some Christian traditions, the book is given to the congregation to kiss, so that in this way they too may show their love of God and God's word.

reading in the Liturgy of the Word, it often determines the reading or readings that precede it. Not only does the gospel tell us about something that Jesus said or did in the past, but the words with which we respond to its message suggest that Christ's presence is somehow made real as we hear the gospel proclaimed: 'Glory to you, O Lord . . . Praise to you, O Christ'. We praise the living Christ directly, acknowledging his presence with us.

After the gospel there is often a sermon and usually a creed. Each is important in itself, but their position in the liturgy suggests that neither stands independently of the readings that precede it. The sermon offers an opportunity for the preacher to make scripture topical, and to make connections between it and the everyday life of the congregation who hear it proclaimed in their midst. It also, together with the Creed, provides a framework in which the particular passages that are the readings for the day should be heard, for part of the role of the preacher is to place the readings in the context (both of a particular book of the Bible, and of the Bible as a whole) from which they are taken. But sermon and creed are each grounded in and dependent on the gospel message that is prior to them both.

Just as the gospels and their message shape the first part of the eucharist, so too they underpin the second, the Liturgy of the Sacrament. The eucharistic prayer climaxes with our thanks for what God has done in Christ, as set out most fully in the gospels, and the risen Jesus' invitation to come to his table points both to the Last Supper and to the other meals that the gospels record Jesus as sharing with others. Here, as we approach the table and receive Jesus' body and blood, his presence may be made real as it was also made real in the reading of the gospel: 'The Lord is here . . . His Spirit is with us.' Here we may eat with Jesus just as did both disciples and sinners in the three gospels that record the Last Supper in a eucharistic way and present it in terms that echo other meal scenes that they also include.

The gospels that we read

Christians and others who have grown up with the four gospels that are bound together at the beginning of the New Testament are not always aware that these four gospels are part of a much larger body of texts that was composed by early Christians. Yet only these four were accepted as authoritative biographical accounts of the impact and significance of Jesus, which is why they alone are included in the Bible. Other gospels may perhaps tell us something about the historical Jesus (although most, if not all, are almost certainly later than, and at least partially dependent upon their canonical counterparts) and are important evidence in the historical study of early Christianity. But they have not been recognized as containing testimony to Jesus that is consistent with the gospel message that underpins the different texts that would come to be recognized as Christian scripture and therefore included in the New Testament canon. Other gospels were never formally excluded from the New Testament canon; they never gained sufficiently wide acceptance to have been included in the first place. Thus, it is primarily for theological, not for historical, reasons that Christians do not consider them to be scripture nor read them in our worship today.

But why is it that we read not one gospel but four? This again is something that Christians today take for granted. Yet it was not always so. Paul writes that there is only one gospel message (Galatians 1.7), and some Christians seem to have thought that there should only have been one gospel book as well. What better way could there be to remain faithful to the gospel proclaimed by Paul, to safeguard the purity of the gospel message, and to deal with non-Christian critics who made much of apparent contradictions between different gospel books? One second-century Christian who appears to have acted on this impulse was Marcion, who used only what appears to have been a shorter version of Luke and to which he referred only as the Gospel. Another was Tatian, who appears to have woven together most of the material contained in Matthew, Mark, Luke and John, such that it formed one continuous whole. Each of these texts used by Marcion and Tatian continued to be influential for many years, but neither won the day. Neither Marcion's Gospel, nor Tatian's Diatessaron (as his harmony was called) were taken up by most Christians, who used instead the four gospels that we continue to use today.

That is why we, like most Christians who have preceded us, read (or hear read to us) neither the work of one gospel writer alone, nor an edited gospel harmony that weaves together in one continuous whole the work of several others. What we read (or hear read) are four discrete accounts that we approach as one fourfold gospel. The theological conviction that underpins this approach, and

GOSPELS

is set out at length by a second-century bishop of Lyons named Irenaeus, can be seen very clearly in the uniform titles that were given to the four canonical gospels at a very early stage in their transmission: 'the Gospel according to Matthew', '... Mark', '... Luke', '... John'. There is only one gospel, but it is recorded in four authoritative texts. There is only one gospel, but it has been recorded by four authoritative witnesses on whose testimony we may rely. There is but one gospel of Jesus Christ, but it is presented in four complementary forms: the (one) gospel according to Matthew, Mark, Luke and John.

Given that we have four canonical gospels, the question arises as to how best they may be read in church, in a liturgical setting in which their different perspectives are considered to complement, not to compete with, each other. At least three answers have been given. One is to move between passages from different gospels, taking texts from all four accounts and reading them in the light of each other and of other parts of scripture. This, broadly speaking, was the approach of the two-year cycle of readings contained in the *Alternative Service Book* (ASB), which was used in the Church of England alongside *The Book of Common Prayer* in the years 1980–2000. Another approach would be a four-year cycle in which each year would include readings from one gospel. This suggestion was made by the Joint Liturgical Group (composed mainly of British liturgical scholars), who published such a lectionary in 1992. However, the approach that has gained most acceptance is based on a three-year cycle, as found (with slight variations) in the Roman Catholic Lectionary for Mass (1969), the Revised

Common Lectionary (1992) and its Church of England version, the *Common Worship* Lectionary (1997).

Undergirding the three-year lectionary is the conviction that Matthew, Mark and Luke should each be read for a year at a time, and that each should be read alongside John. (John, we may note, is often referred to as the fourth gospel, thus setting it apart from the other three. Matthew, Mark, and Luke are often referred to as the synoptic gospels, because the pattern of similarities and differences that they share shows that they present Jesus from a broadly similar perspective, and means that they may therefore be read 'syn-optically' or alongside each other.) This gives the three synoptic gospels an apparently dominant place, but ensures that their presentation of Jesus is never too far removed from the often quite different perspective offered by John. This approach is not without its problems, and it can sometimes seem frustrating when the lectionary switches suddenly from a synoptic gospel to John, as for example at Easter. Yet the advantages of reading John in close proximity to the synoptic accounts may be greater than the drawbacks. This pattern allows us to hear how John seems sometimes to offer different perspectives on events that are familiar to us from the synoptic accounts. It also means that we can hear how sometimes John seems to take further claims that the other gospel writers make, or how he makes similar claims in quite different ways.

Also, John's gospel often works by making related points again and again, and was probably written to be read in much longer sections than we are accustomed to hearing read today. Therefore reading it in short sections over the course of most of a year would probably diminish rather than increase the prospect that its distinctive voice would be heard, and might also set it too far apart from the perspectives of Matthew, Mark and Luke. Thus, there is much to be said for the recurrent juxtaposition of John and the synoptic gospels, for this approach to reading the gospels offers a potentially fruitful dynamic that might easily be lost were John allocated a year of his own.

The producers of the Revised Common Lectionary explain their approach like this:

> The lectionary provides a three-year plan or pattern for the Sunday readings. Each year is centred on one of the synoptic gospels. Year A is the year of Matthew, Year B is the year of Mark, and Year C is the year of Luke. John is read each year, especially in the times around Christmas, Lent and Easter, and also in the year of Mark, whose gospel is shorter than the others. The three synoptic evangelists have particular insights into Christ. Each year, we allow one of these gospels to lead us to Christ by a semicontinuous reading during the Sundays in Ordinary Time. Passages and parables that are unique to one evangelist are normally included as part of the Sunday readings ... The Revised Common Lectionary seeks to read the four gospels during the liturgy in a manner which respects their own varied literary structures.[55]

---

[55] The Consultation on Common Texts, 1992, *The Revised Common Lectionary*, Nashville/Norwich: Abingdon Press/Canterbury Press, pp. 13, 16.

'The three synoptic evangelists have particular insights into Christ' note these scholars, and much has been written on what these insights include, and how we might respond to them today. This brief essay offers little opportunity to discuss at any length what the particular insights of each gospel writer might be, but readers who wish to pursue this matter will find a wide range of helpful books that do just that.[56]

The gospels and other readings

I have touched on the way in which a three-year lectionary can appear to give a dominant place to the synoptic gospels at John's expense, but have argued that this need not be the case. Another charge that might be raised against the prominence of the gospels in the lectionary is that the emphasis that we place upon them distorts our approach to the Bible as a whole. The gospels make up only a small proportion of the Christian Bible, yet they are read at every eucharist, whereas much of the rest of the Bible is omitted altogether. Furthermore, other bits of the Bible are sometimes selected because they fit with the gospel readings. Thus, once again the lectionary's emphasis on the gospels may distort our approach to the Bible, for even when we read from the Old Testament

---

56 Good starting places on all four gospels include Stephen C. Barton, 2006, *The Cambridge Companion to the Gospels*, Cambridge: Cambridge University Press; Stephen C. Barton, 1992, *The Spirituality of the Gospels,* London: SPCK; Richard A. Burridge, 2005, *Four Gospels, One Jesus?* London: SPCK; Andrew Gregory, ed., 2006, *The Fourfold Gospel Commentary*, London: SPCK.

or the rest of the New Testament, we sometimes do so through the lenses of the gospels.[57]

The *Common Worship* Lectionary, it must be said, is less susceptible to this criticism than is the Revised Common Lectionary, which in turn is less susceptible to this criticism than the Roman Catholic Lectionary for Mass on which it is based. Two examples may illustrate this point. First, the Revised Common Lectionary allows for semicontinuous reading of parts of the Old Testament after Pentecost, thus allowing not insignificant portions of Old Testament narrative to be read on their own terms. Here its Protestant compilers consciously provide an alternative to the way in which at this point the Roman Catholic Lectionary offers only Old Testament readings that fit with the gospel for each Sunday. Second, the compilers of the *Common Worship* Lectionary note that the Revised Common Lectionary provides surprisingly little attention to creation, so they draw on Genesis 1 and 2 to provide for a 'Creation Sunday' on the second Sunday before Lent. This is a good example of how the compilers of the lectionary have had to move away from the dominance of the gospels in order to address a major biblical and doctrinal topic on which the gospels are largely silent.

Underlying this criticism is a question about the extent to which Christians should give the gospels a privileged place as a canon within the canon. This may be raised

---

57 See John Goldingay, 1999, 'Canon and lection', in Bryan D. Spinks and Iain R. Torrance, eds., *To Glorify God: Essays on Modern Reformed Liturgies*, Edinburgh: T&T Clark, pp. 85–97, see pp. 92–97.

for what might be considered theological reasons. For example, there may be a desire to maintain an emphasis on the doctrine of justification, or on other teachings that are associated primarily with the letters of Paul, not with the gospels. It may also be for liturgical reasons, such as the wish to provide a lectionary for settings that are not eucharistic. Thus, for example, the Anglican services of Morning and Evening Prayer have tended to give equal weighting to readings from the Old and New Testaments, and to give a prominent place to the psalms. Should the psalms not be read on their own terms and in a systematic way, then much of the range of material that they offer is effectively lost from Christian worship.[58]

A third reason, which we might call historical, may also be given. This is that the first scriptures on which the followers of Jesus drew were those that Christians now call the Old Testament, and that these were quite sufficient for the initial needs of those who followed Jesus. Not only that, the letters of Paul were almost certainly written, and at least some of them may have been circulating together, before the four gospels were written. There was living faith in Jesus, and Jesus' followers assembled for worship, before the gospels were written. The earliest Christians had the Jewish scriptures alone as their sacred books and only with time did Christian writings, the canonical gospels among them, take on an equal or greater status than the writings of the Jewish Bible. Even in the mid-second century, a theologian such

---

58 Goldingay, 'Canon and lection', p. 95.

as Justin Martyr, who almost certainly knew Matthew and Luke, and may also have known Mark and John, preferred to outline the story of Jesus by reference to the Jewish Bible, not by reference to the gospels.

Yet today, in our public worship for much of the year, those Jewish scriptures – the Christian Old Testament – are used only to cast light on the gospels. This appears to be almost the opposite of what took place when the gospels were first written and read. At that time the gospels were shaped not only by the impact that Jesus had on the lives of those who encountered him, but also by the way in which those early disciples viewed that impact through the prism of their understanding of Jewish scripture and shaped their narratives accordingly. The gospels could not have been written were it not for the Old Testament, so any neglect of its writings has profound effects on our understanding of the gospels.

Of course, later Christians cannot – and should not seek to – return to the historical circumstances of the earliest followers of Jesus. We cannot live as if we were in the same historical context that they were. Nevertheless, it is important to note the extent to which our emphasis on the gospels may in fact sideline and displace the very scriptures that were of such importance in forming both the outlook and understanding of the gospel writers and also the gospels that they wrote. Is this what the compilers of the lectionary set out to do, or could it be an unexpected and unwelcome consequence of their approach? By downplaying the importance of the Old Testament, do we deprive ourselves of the very texts that we need to know if we are to understand the gospels as fully as we can? That is a very real danger, but the answer may lie less in taking away from the centrality of the gospel in the eucharist and more in the realization that Christians need to make sure that the diet of scripture that they encounter both in the liturgy and elsewhere is not their only exposure to Christian scripture as transmitted in both the Old Testament and the New. We need to read the whole Bible, both the Old Testament and the New, for ourselves.

Further, it is also important to be aware of why the compilers of the lectionary put such emphasis on the gospels, for it brings us to the heart – but not the totality – of Christian claims about God's activity in his world. The Revised Common Lectionary, they write,

> allows the sequence of gospel readings each year to lead God's people to a deeper knowledge of Christ and faith in him. It is the paschal mystery of the saving death and resurrection of the Lord Jesus that is proclaimed through the lectionary readings and the preaching of the Church.[59]

Neither the lectionary readings, nor the preaching of the church should be *limited to* 'the paschal mystery of the saving death and resurrection of the Lord Jesus'. But this does not mean that they may not be given the central place in the celebration of the eucharist and therefore in the life of the worshipping church. Christian

---

59 The Consultation on Common Texts, *The Revised Common Lectionary*, p. 12. But see Goldingay, 'Canon and lection', p. 94.

worshippers may need to engage more fully with scripture than they do in the eucharist, and certainly they do need to remember that they are to engage both with life and with scripture as they actually are, in all their messiness and diversity. But this does not mean that a gospel-based Christological focus is inappropriate at the heart of Christian worship, even if it does mean that it should not be the only context in which Christians come together to worship, think, pray and be empowered to live as part of Christ's broken body in the broken world for which God gave his only Son.

The promise of presence

Given the centrality of the saving death and resurrection of Jesus both in the celebration of the eucharist and in Christian life more generally, it is hardly a surprise that the gospels play such an important role in the eucharist. Nor should it be a surprise that they are seen as revelatory texts that make the risen Jesus' presence known among those who worship him today. We have noted already how this expectation is implied in the acclamations made when the gospel is read ('Glory to you, O Lord . . . Praise to you, O Christ') but it is also worth noting how the content of the gospels supports our belief that Christ is present when Christian people gather in Christ's name and remember what he said and did. Thus in the remainder of this chapter I will move from talking *about* the gospels and their place in the eucharist to looking at what they actually say, and how that might be relevant to the way in which we approach them.

In the Gospel according to Matthew, we find clear foundations for the belief that Jesus is present with his followers, especially when they come together in his name (18.20). At the beginning of the gospel, Jesus is introduced as Emmanuel, God with us (1.23). This is the same Jesus, now risen from the dead, who promises the disciples that he will be with them every day, to the end of the age (28.20). Thus, at the end of Matthew's gospel it is made clear that God, as known in Jesus, remains present with those who did not have the opportunity to meet Jesus in the flesh but nevertheless know his presence as they follow his commandments and teach others to do the same.

This promise of Jesus' presence among the disciples knows no boundaries and extends to everything that they do, but Matthew also links this presence to settings that have to do with worship. Jesus is greater than the temple (12.6), where previously God's presence was primarily to be found, but now it is to be found where two or three gather together in Jesus' name (18.20). Thus, also in the middle of Matthew's gospel, in the very place where the evangelist speaks twice of the church, and the way in which its members should behave towards one another (18.15–20), Matthew stresses that Jesus is the one in whom God's presence is to be found, and that Jesus is present among those who meet in his name. Put in the context of Christian reflection on the eucharist, what this perhaps suggests is that Jesus' presence is to be known not only when bread and wine are taken, broken, given and consumed as Jesus is remembered, but also that Jesus' presence is to be discerned more widely – not just in the eucharist, but wherever believers are assembled (18.20) and wherever they may go as they make disciples and baptize them in the threefold name (28.19–20).

Matthew does not make the point explicitly, but it is hard to see how Jesus' command to teach others to obey all that he has commanded the disciples could not involve passing on the content of the gospel that Matthew himself has written. This is also implied at 23.13, where Jesus states clearly that the proclamation of the gospel will mean that what an unnamed woman has just done will be told in remembrance of her. But it is elsewhere in the gospels, most notably in Luke, that we see one of the gospel writers showing how the reading and explaining of scripture was an important element in Jewish worship and in the life of the early followers of Jesus. Luke's narrative, we are told, is written so that he (presumably a follower of Jesus already) may know the truth of the things concerning which Theophilus has already been instructed. As does John (John 20.30–31), Luke makes clear that he writes not just to provide information, but to show that the information given may be trusted and may transform the lives of those who hear the good news conveyed.

Typical of Luke is a keenness to show that the later practice of Jesus' followers is grounded in, and reflects, the practice of Jesus himself. Thus, when they 'devoted themselves to the apostles' teaching and common life, to the breaking of bread and the prayers' (Acts 2.42), or when Paul taught them before they broke bread (Acts 20.7), Jesus' disciples were doing what they had learned from him. Three passages in Luke's gospel support this point. The first two may be mentioned only briefly. One is the scene in the synagogue at Nazareth (Luke 4.16–30), which Luke uses to introduce and to set the scene for Jesus' public ministry in Galilee. Jesus not only reads from scripture, but declares that it is fulfilled in the presence of those listening to the reading. There is nothing eucharistic about this passage, but it points to the importance of the reading and preaching of scripture in the ministry of Jesus, and offers a vivid example of how God's word is actually made real and effective as it is read in a worshipping community: 'Today this scripture has been fulfilled in your hearing' (Luke 4.21).

In the second passage, Luke's account of the Last Supper (Luke 22.14–20), the eucharistic context is clear. Jesus not only takes, thanks God for, and gives bread and wine to his disciples, but also explicitly tells them to 'do this in remembrance of me'. Luke's account both refers to something that happened in the past and relates it to the present and the future. It also includes Jesus' teaching – both in explanation of what he is doing with the bread and the wine, and in response to the subsequent squabbling of the disciples (22.24–30). As at Nazareth, teaching takes place in a setting in which those who have gathered acknowledge God's presence with them, and in which what the scriptures have said about Jesus is fulfilled (24.37; cf. 4.21).

All three elements – Jesus' teaching, the emphasis on the fulfilment of scripture and a eucharistic context – are present in the third passage, Luke's account of the risen Jesus' encounter with two disciples on the road to Emmaus.

Returning to the road to Emmaus

This story is the second of two episodes in which Luke recounts for the gospel's readers the story of the first Easter Day. In it Luke shows how through the explanation of scripture and the breaking of bread two disciples move from despair to hope, from disappointment and dejection to a renewed belief in God's work in the world. Luke writes, of course, at a time when Jesus had long since ceased to appear physically to the disciples as happened on that Easter Day. Luke makes clear that he never met the earthly Jesus, so his perspective is similar to our own. We know that the ascended Jesus is no longer physically present here on earth, and Luke writes for people like us. Luke knows that Jesus will not appear to others as he appeared to those on the road to Emmaus. So the evangelist tells the story in such a way to show that we too may believe, even if the reality of Jesus' presence with us can be known only without a physical presence by our sides.

Central to this account are two of the ways in which Jesus may be known today. One is through understanding the scriptures (Luke 24.25–27, 32). The other is in the breaking of the bread (Luke 24.30–31, 35). Through them both, Luke suggests, Jesus makes his presence known.

When Cleopas and the other unnamed disciple set out for Emmaus, their hearts and minds are filled with disappointment and despair. Turned in on themselves, they try to figure out the meaning of all that has happened. Deep in earnest conversation, their eyes are kept from recognizing Jesus when he draws alongside. What are you talking about, Jesus asks; and for those of us who read the gospel, the dramatic irony in their reply is unmistakeable. It is these two travellers who do not realize that it is Jesus to whom they speak, yet they accuse him of not knowing what has happened. It is these two travellers who have given up on their cherished hope that Jesus would redeem Israel, yet this is what the one to whom they speak has done.

Cleopas and his companion had heard that Jesus had been raised. But they did not believe, and their focus remained on his death – on his humiliating and agonizing death as seen in the abject horror of the cross. They did not understand Jesus' death as an act of redemption. They did not understand Jesus' death as a means of entering into glory. They understand Jesus' death in the only way, humanly speaking, that it could be understood: as a public and miserable failure for all in Jerusalem to see. God could not work like this. Or so, it appears, they believed. How could a prophet mighty in word and deed come to an end like this? How could God let us down?

How foolish you are, Jesus tells them. You may know the scriptures, but you fail to see what they say. Nothing that has happened need call into question your conviction that Jesus was a prophet powerful in word and deed. What you need to question are your preconceived ideas of how God's prophet and thus how God might act.

Would that we knew the particular scriptures to which Jesus might have referred at this point, but here

GOSPELS

Luke gives us no clues. Reading scripture backwards, reading our Old Testament in light of our New, then it is hard for us not to think that passages like Isaiah 53 would have been prominent (as it is later in Luke's two volumes: see Acts 8.32–35). Yet Luke's point seems to be that *the whole* of scripture (Luke 24.27) points to Jesus and to the cross and resurrection. That the whole pattern of God's activity points to, foreshadows and culminates in the suffering and glorification of God's Son. That here in Jesus' selfless self-giving we see what God is truly like. That here in Jesus' resurrection we see God acting to vindicate the beloved one; to endorse all that Jesus has done; to point to Jesus as the one in whom God now judges the world. Those who crucified Jesus got the verdict wrong: now God acts to overturn their mistake!

Jesus takes texts with which the disciples are familiar, but shows them how to read them in a different way. To see with fresh eyes what was always there but that they could not see before. And yet. And yet it appears that it made no difference. They continue along the road, but the penny of recognition has not yet dropped. Approaching Emmaus, Jesus makes to go on further but at their entreaties stops to stay with them.

And then, unexpectedly, it happens. At the table, the penny drops. Jesus takes bread, gives thanks, and breaking the bread he gives it to them. They recognize their companion, and as soon as they do so, Jesus vanishes from their sight. This is the climax of the story. The moment when they recognize Jesus. The moment when they experience for themselves that Jesus is alive and present with them. The moment to which they refer when they rush back to tell the others in Jerusalem. 'Then they told them what had happened on the road, and how he had been made known to them in the breaking of the bread' (Luke 24.35).

This phrase, 'the breaking of the bread', is important – both in a eucharistic context, and in the context of Luke's two-volume work. When next Luke uses the phrase, early in Acts, it is to describe one of the distinctive features of the life of the early church. The early Christians were those 'who devoted themselves to the apostles' teaching and common life, to the breaking of bread and the prayers' (Acts 2.42).

Of course, this does not mean that Jesus actually celebrated the eucharist on the road to Emmaus. That would be to push the text too far. But the eucharistic language seems unmistakeable, and appears to be the point that Luke is making. What Christians of Luke's day did when they gathered at the table was not altogether different from what happened at Emmaus, for they too could have the living Jesus made known to them in the breaking of the bread.

Just like us, Christians of Luke's day could not see the risen Christ physically present with them. But we, like them, can have the living Jesus made known to us in the breaking of the bread. Jesus was present throughout the journey to Emmaus, yet the disciples on the way could not see him. They experienced the presence of Jesus in the breaking of the bread, and it was then that all else fell into place. They recognized Jesus in the breaking of the bread, and it was in the light of that encounter that they realized how their hearts had burned within them when their companion interpreted the scriptures to them. Their minds had been informed, their hearts had been touched, but they only realized in the breaking of the bread.

On one level, Luke's story is that of the transformation of two individuals. On another, it is the story of how Christians may still encounter Jesus and learn to see Jesus as more than merely a stranger and fellow traveller. How we may move into insight, from despair to delight. The risen Jesus is ascended, but it is this physical absence that allows for a universal presence by the Spirit. For in the reading of scripture, and in the breaking of bread, the risen one continues to be present though unseen.

Only when they knew Jesus in the breaking of the bread did the disciples on the journey to Emmaus understand why their hearts had burned within them. Had they but understood before, they would have known Jesus' presence even though they could not see it. Once again, Luke writes for people like us. We cannot see Jesus, yet there may be moments when our hearts burn within us on account of the presence of the risen Jesus walking with us, calling us to be companions. The risen Jesus teaching us to see in scripture what we had not seen before. The risen Jesus inviting us to table-fellowship where we 'proclaim the Lord's death until he comes' (cf. 1 Corinthians 11.26). Where the risen Jesus invite others to join with us in receiving all that he longs to give. It is for this reason that we draw near with faith, that we respond to the invitation that Jesus gives.

Perhaps for us, as for Cleopas and the other disciple, it is when we encounter the risen one in the breaking of the bread that God most fully gives us the grace to understand what God's word might be saying to us today. Thus Luke's gospel supports the conviction that it is when scripture is heard and received by those who gather round the Christ's table that God's voice may be most clearly heard.

Appendix 1

A note on using this book to support preaching

Christian people think their thoughts in constant interaction with scripture, which Anglican tradition – sustained by the practice of daily prayer – encourages us to engage daily. Each author in this volume makes reference to a number of scripture passages to shape and support their reflections. And it may be that readers who are preachers wish to engage the themes of this volume in their preaching ministry (not least at a time when the 'sacramental belonging' of children is being enlarged to include their full participation in the eucharist, and the challenges and opportunities of inviting children's participation sometimes requires robust catechesis for the young and their elders alike). The following notes suggest options for drawing out the eucharistic themes of this volume in preaching at the eucharist.

Lectionary provisions and permissions

In the Church of England, 'following the lectionary' involves considerable freedoms, and these are often not appreciated. Although 'authorized lectionary provision

APPENDIX I

[is] not matter for local decision except where that provision permits',[60] that 'except' permits wide variation: *Common Worship* outlines the rule that during the Christmas cycle (from Advent Sunday through to Candlemas) and the Easter cycle (from Ash Wednesday through to Pentecost) and on Trinity Sunday and All Saints' Day, the prescribed readings must be used.[61] However, outside those times – all of 'ordinary time' and, therefore, a majority of each year – local lectionaries may be produced 'for pastoral reasons or preaching or teaching purposes'.[62] The creation of a local scripture reading scheme requires 'consultation' between the parish church council and minister, but is entirely permissible. Furthermore, *New Patterns for Worship* suggests some avenues of departure from the 'set' readings, and models the construction of local reading and sermon series. 'Section C' of *New Patterns for Worship*, the teaching resource for the *Common Worship* range, provides numerous forms of 'modular Bible readings'.[63] These tend to focus in on particular canonical books or portions of books, or take thematic approaches to particular subjects. *New Patterns for Worship* suggests that churches constructing local lectionaries 'should ensure that an adequate amount of Scripture is chosen; that justice is done to the balance of the book and to the general teaching of Scripture; that appropriate Gospel passages are included if the services include Holy Com-

---

60 *Common Worship*, p. 332.
61 *Common Worship*, p. 540.
62 *Common Worship*, p. 540.
63 *New Patterns for Worship*, pp. 98–122.

munion; and that the PCC or an appropriate lay group is involved in the decisions'.[64] These are good guidelines to bear in mind in constructing local patterns of reading to help congregations explore the meanings of the eucharist, as anything else.

Jo Bailey Wells places emphasis on the Passover as a model for Christians at eucharist, hence the Passover account from Exodus 12.21–27 would make an appropriate Old Testament reading. A psalm associated with Passover might also be used, such as Psalm 116.12–19. A New Testament reading such as Revelation 4.1–11 could be connected to Jo's emphasis on the 'five acts' of biblical 'drama', and her point that Christians are privileged to know 'how the play ends'. This extract from Revelation also echoes the vision of Isaiah, which Jo quotes along the way in her chapter and with which she draws it to an evocative conclusion. Mark 14.12–16, 22–26 sets the Last Supper in the context of the Passover and so could be used to draw in Jo's themes.

Gordon Mursell has chosen as his main focus a psalm that is not a major feature of the lectionary, and his chapter makes no references to New Testament material. Old Testament material such as Proverbs 9.1–16, on the glory of wisdom, or Deuteronomy 8.2–3, 14b–16a, the story of divine provision of manna in the desert, might be used. Psalm 73 is, of course, the obvious psalm. From the New Testament, a text such as Romans 8.26–39 might be used in that it appeals to the sense that the Spirit helps us to pray, and conveys conviction of the

---

64 *New Patterns for Worship*, p. 106.

APPENDIX I

overwhelming presence of divine love. The psalms as help to prayer and Psalm 73's celebration of intimacy with God find some resonance in this Romans extract, which is luminous in its own right. A gospel passage such as Mark 15.33–39 may make a compelling gospel reading in this sequence – not least following the Romans text – in that it shows Jesus' use of the psalms, here in extremis.

Joy Tetley refers to Jeremiah 31.31–34, which is itself quoted in the Letter to the Hebrews, the focus of her chapter. She refers also to Psalm 51, which she associates with the Collect for Purity (a prayer to which Jo Bailey Wells also draws attention). Psalm 51.1–12 picks up key resonances with that prayer. Hebrews 4.12–16 is a major feature of Joy's chapter, making it an obvious choice from the New Testament, although the point that Joy makes about Hebrews being comparatively neglected is reflected in the fact that it is represented at best patchily in the lectionary, and so underrepresented texts from the letter might also well be drawn in. *New Patterns for Worship* suggests ways of raising the profile of Hebrews in Christian assembly.[65] John 17.20–26 could be used as a gospel, given that Joy refers to this chapter of the fourth gospel, and that Jesus' prayer remembered there is oftentimes referred to as his 'high priestly prayer', a point that might readily be associated with Joy's explorations of the theme of Jesus as high priest.

Isaiah 61.1–4 might be used as an Old Testament reading associated with Andrew Gregory's chapter,

---

65 *New Patterns for Worship*, p. 122.

A NOTE ON USING THIS BOOK

given that Andrew refers to Luke 4's memory of Jesus' preaching in the synagogue when Jesus reads this prophecy from Isaiah. Psalm 31.1–5 shows Jesus' use of the psalms, as recorded in the gospels (and such use of the psalms in this lectionary sequence would complement that suggested in the sequence related to Gordon's reflections). Andrew refers to Acts 2.42, hence Acts 2.42–47 might make an appropriate New Testament reading. Luke 24.13–35 is the obvious choice of gospel reading in light of Andrew's argument, though Luke 4.16–20 would serve as an alternative (perhaps especially if the Emmaus memory was much used in explorations of reflections in the first volume of *Renewing the Eucharist – Journey*).

Appendix 2

Sample questions for reflection and conversation

Common Worship indicates that 'the term "sermon" includes less formal exposition, the use of drama, interviews, discussion, audio-visuals and the insertion of hymns or other sections of the service between parts of the sermon' which may come before or after one of the readings or prayers.[66] In each case, the sermon (in the narrow sense) is only one means of engaging the word, and a whole ecology of ways of appropriating and responding to scripture is suggested. This kind of diversification of means of communication and appropriation is increasingly important in order to help people to hear and respond to the scriptures. Yet this in itself may not be enough. Home groups and study groups, and in some places all-age Sunday school classes of some kind may be essential to support lifelong learning in the faith. The following are intended as *examples* of questions that might be used or adapted in discussions in home groups and all-age Sunday schools – or, in contexts where it is appropriate, as beginnings to discussion that may complement or

---

66 See *Common Worship*, p. 27; cf. p. 332 (note 'on occasion').

SAMPLE QUESTIONS

replace a monological sermon. The questions may also be used by individual readers to focus their engagement with particular chapters in this collection. They are certainly not the only questions that might be asked, and they may well not be 'right' for certain contexts; rather, they are intended as an encouragement to readers to 'mine' the material in this book for themselves.

Hebrew scripture

1. Jo invites understanding of rituals as participation in the scriptures. Do you have, or can you imagine, experience of this?
2. Jo turns a number of phrases to suggest that imaginative reading of scripture may help us to indwell knowledge of God – playing ourselves into outworking of God's story/sensing God's story from the inside/taking our part in a divine drama. What do you think?
3. (How) do you put your 'heart' into Bible reading?
4. Jo is confident that the Old Testament can help contemporary Christians to 'treasure every priceless voice', especially quieter and more hesitant ones. What do you make of this idea?

Psalms

1. Gordon stresses corporate and individual experience, and ways the psalms relate to both. How do you think of your experience?

2. Gordon emphasizes lament – a genre of prayer often missing from public worship. How might it help?
3. Gordon speaks of the psalms making good 'rucksack prayers' – 'spiritual resources we can carry with us on our journeys through life'. What are your rucksack resources, and are psalms part of them?
4. Gordon points out that the lectionary privileges psalms among the Old Testament as it privileges gospels among the New Testament. Do you find this idea helpful, and how?

New Testament

1. Joy stresses that liturgy is shot through with scripture. Had you noticed, and how might you appreciate this feature of worship?
2. Joy writes of 'total exposure to God', deep knowing and being known. How does worship help you face this idea?
3. Joy speaks of the priesthood of Jesus in terms of God's determined yearning that all should know God, with free and confident access into the divine presence. How might you begin to make sense of the 'priesthood' of Jesus?
4. Joy writes of pain and joy being 'inseparably linked' in God's passion for the world. (How) can you relate to this?

Gospels

1. Andrew stresses the importance of the Emmaus story. Have you thought about it?

SAMPLE QUESTIONS

2. Andrew writes of four discrete accounts of Jesus that we approach as one 'fourfold gospel'. What do you make of the idea of a 'fourfold gospel'?
3. Andrew points out both promise and problems with the gospels' centrality in the lectionary. Do you see more problems or more promise?
4. Andrew thinks that Christians do well to engage the Bible beyond the liturgy more fully than the lectionary allows. How might you pick up this idea?

About the Contributors

Andrew Gregory is Chaplain and Fellow of University College, Oxford University. His publications include *The Reception of Luke and Acts in the Period Before Irenaeus* (2003), *The Reception of the New Testament in the Apostolic Fathers* (co-editor with Christopher Tuckett) (2005), *Trajectories Through the New Testament and the Apostolic Fathers* (co-editor with Christopher Tuckett) (2005), and *The Fourfold Gospel Commentary* (editor) (2006).

Gordon Mursell is Bishop of Stafford. His publications include *Out of the Deep: Prayer as Protest* (1989), *The Story of Christian Spirituality: Two Thousand Years, from East to West* (editor) (2001), *English Spirituality: From Earliest Times to 1700* (2001), *English Spirituality: From 1700 to the Present Day* (2001) and *Praying in Exile* (2005).

Joy Tetley is an Anglican priest based in Oxford, who exercises a ministry of prayer, writing and teaching. She was formerly Archdeacon of Worcester. Her publications include *Encounter with God in Hebrews* (1995) and *A Rebellious Prophet: Jonah* (2003).

ABOUT THE CONTRIBUTORS

Jo Bailey Wells is Associate Professor of the Practice of Christian Ministry and Bible at Duke University, North Carolina, USA. Her publications include *God's Holy People: A Theme in Biblical Theology* (2000) and *Isaiah: A Bible Commentary for Every Day* (2006).

Stephen Burns is Research Fellow in Public and Contextual Theology at United Theological College, Charles Sturt University, Sydney, Australia. His publications include *Worship in Context: Liturgical Theology, Children and the City* (2006), *Liturgy* (SCM Studyguide) (2006), *Exchanges of Grace: Essays in Honour of Ann Loades* (co-editor with Natalie K. Watson) (2008), *The Edge of God: New Liturgical Texts and Contexts in Conversation* (co-editor with Nicola Slee and Michael N. Jagessar) (2008) and *Christian Worship in Australia: Inculturating the Liturgical Tradition* (co-editor with Anita Monro) (2009).

The leading Christian newspaper for less than the price of a coffee!

From the erudite to the everyday, from the inspiring to the irreverent, from the vital to the silly, the *Church Times* keeps you fully informed each week of everything new in the Church and its relationship with the world

For just £65, the *Church Times* will be delivered direct to your door, every week for a year. You will also gain **free access** to all online content and the *Church Times* archive via our website **www.churchtimes.co.uk**

Order now — quote 'CT0930'

Phone: 01603 612914; email: subs@churchtimes.co.uk
or write to Church Times Subscriptions,
Hymns Ancient & Modern Ltd, St Mary's Works
St Mary's Plain, Norwich NR3 3BH

Or contact us for a **free sample copy**